# A Practical Guide to Planning Law and Rights of Way in National Parks, the Broads and AONBs

**James Maurici QC** is a barrister at Landmark Chambers. He has particular expertise in advising and acting in respect of development affecting National Parks and AONBs and in relation to habitats and air quality issues. He is the author of the so-called Maurici opinions on the meaning of "major development" in National Parks. He promoted the South Downs National Park Local Plan with James Neill.

**James Neill** is planning barrister of over 14 years' experience, with particular expertise in the regulatory framework affecting development in National Parks, SSSIs and AONBs.

**Stephen Morgan** has specialised in planning and related fields of law. His experience, both as adviser and advocate, covers the range of planning and related topics. His work covers the regulatory aspects (under the various regimes and Directives) as well as the planning issues.

**Stephen Whale** has over 20 years of experience in planning law, rights of way, commons, forestry and village greens. In July 2020 the Secretary of State for Environment, Food and Rural Affairs appointed Stephen as a Member of the South Downs National Park Authority.

**Kate Olley** is a specialist planning and public law with over 20 years' experience, advising in relation to development affecting AONBs and in all areas of planning and infrastructure.

**Jacqueline Lean** has a cross-discipline practice, encompassing property, planning and public law, as well as environmental law matters related to those areas of practice. She has particular experience in infrastructure projects within, or affecting, National Parks and AONBs, and public rights of way.

**Matthew Dale-Harris** grew up in the South Downs with cousins on Exmoor and has a longstanding affection for all things National Park. His bar work focuses on planning, property and environmental law with particular expertise in dealing with habitats issues and the SSSI regime.

**Nick Grant** was called to the Bar in 2016, and practises in in planning, property, and environmental law. He specialises in sectors and issues which touch on all three disciplines, as National Parks, AONBs, the Broads, and their associated rights and requirements.

# A Practical Guide to Planning Law and Rights of Way in National Parks, the Broads and AONBs


James Maurici Q.C. BA (Hons), BCL (Oxon)
Barrister, Inner Temple

James Neill MA (Oxon) Lit. Hum., Dip. Law
Barrister, Inner Temple

Stephen Morgan LLB (Hons), MA (Environmental Planning)
Barrister, Gray's Inn

Stephen Whale B.Soc.Sc. (Birmingham), Dip.Law
Barrister, Gray's Inn

Kate Olley MA (Oxon)
Barrister, Middle Temple

Jacqueline Lean BA (Hons) (Cantab), LLM
Barrister, Gray's Inn

Matthew Dale-Harris BA (Hons) MSt
Barrister, Middle Temple

Nick Grant LLB, LLM (Harv)
Barrister, Inner Temple



Law Brief Publishing

Published 2020 by Law Brief Publishing, an imprint of Law Brief Publishing Ltd
30 The Parks
Minehead
Somerset
TA24 8BT

www.lawbriefpublishing.com

Paperback: 978-1-913715-22-9

# FOREWORD

I welcome this new book, which focusses on the legislative and policy provisions that have developed within our planning system, since the 1940s, for the protection of the most important landscapes in England, Wales and Northern Ireland, including National Parks, Areas of Outstanding Natural Beauty and the Norfolk and Suffolk Broads. The planning issues that arise when development is proposed in these very special landscapes can be unusual and sometimes complex.

These areas cover a large area of England, Wales and Northern Ireland. Until now there has been no book that has focused on these matters. This book is thus a valuable addition to the resources of those who have to deal with planning and other environmental law issues in such designated areas. The book also looks at topics relating to rights of way and other access rights, as well as issues relating to water, habitats and other matters as they apply in these areas.

In my time as a Judge I had many occasions to look at some of these problems. For example, in Derbyshire Dales DC v Secretary of State for Communities and Local Government [2010] 1 P. & C.R. 19 the Peak District National Park Authority was one of the claimants in respect of the grant on appeal of a wind farm with one of the key issues in play being the impact on the character and appearance of the surrounding landscape including the Peak National Park; and in R (CPRE Kent) v Dover District Council [2018] 1 W.L.R. 108 (in the Supreme Court) the siting of part of the proposed development in the Kent Downs AONB was one of the factors relevant in considering whether reasons were required for the grant of planning permission.

I congratulate the authors (from Landmark Chambers) on this important addition to the planning library.

Lord Carnwath CVO
September 2020

# PREFACE

This edition represents the work of 8 authors and colleagues at Landmark Chambers. It discusses the law as at 1 September 2020. It covers both planning law and the law relating to rights of way and public access. As such we hope it serves as a useful reference guide for practitioners (whether lawyers or otherwise) with an interest in the National Parks and AONBs of England, Wales and Northern Ireland and the Broads.

Planning law and policy is a particularly fast evolving area and the summer of 2020 was no exception in terms of new cases and policy announcements. Only one week before the book was finalised an important case on the Sandford principle (and in fact only the second time the High Court has considered that principle) (Stubbs v Lake District National Park Authority [2020] EWHC 2292 (Admin)) was handed down. We discuss that case in Chapter 1. The wholesale reform of the planning system heralded by the White Paper Planning for the Future is discussed in Chapter 1. We decided that rather than postpone indefinitely and await the outcome of the consultation on those proposals we should press on and complete this edition. We have endeavoured to discuss other anticipated statutory reforms where there was sufficient detail released into the public domain to do so meaningfully. Legislative changes which will impact on the planning functions of National Park Authorities are due soon if and when the Environment Bill (discussed in Chapter 5) is enacted. The end of the Brexit transition period may well see a number of changes to other statutory provisions discussed in that chapter.

We wrote this book in very unusual circumstances given the national lockdown between March and July 2020 due to the global pandemic. The pressure placed on our National Parks and AONBs as that lockdown eased and people flocked to them only served to highlight their national value and the pressures they face, and so the publication of this first edition discussing the law that both protects and allows access to these areas we hope proves timely.

James Maurici et al.
Landmark Chambers
September 2020

# TABLE OF CASES

# TABLE OF LEGISLATION

# ABBREVIATIONS

The following are the main abbreviations used in this book. In each chapter, where the context requires it, some of the abbreviations for the main statutes are set out again for ease of reference.

Legislation (Chronological)

The 1949 Act, or NPAC 1949 – The National Parks and Access to the Countryside Act 1949

The CA 1968 – The Countryside Act 1968

The HA 1980 – The Highways Act 1982

The WCA 1981 – The Wildlife and Countryside Act 1981

The NSBA 1988 – The Norfolk and Suffolk Broads Act 1988

The TCPA 1990 – The Town and Country Planning Act 1990

The EA 1995 – The Environment Act 1995

The CROW 2000, or the 2000 Act – The Countryside and Rights of Way Act 2000

The NERC Act 2006 – The Natural Environment and Rural Communities Act 2006

The PCPA 2004 – The Planning and Compulsory Purchase Act 2004

The PA 2008 – The Planning Act 2008

BAA 2009 – The Broads Authority Act 2000

The PWA 2015 – The Planning (Wales Act) 2015

The DMP Order – The Town and Country Planning (Development Management Procedure) (England) Order 2015/595

Other (Alphabetical)

AONB – Area of Outstanding Natural Beauty

AONB MP – AONB Management Plan

The Glover Review – Landscapes Review, Final Report (2019)

CJEU – Court of Justice of the European Union

LPA – Local Planning Authority

NAAONB – National Association for AONBs

NP – National Park

NPA – National Park Authority

The NP Circular – The English National Parks and the Broads UK Government Vision and Circular 2010 (March 2010)

NPE – National Parks England

NPPF (2012) – the National Planning Policy Framework (2012)

NPPF (2018) – the National Planning Policy Framework (2018)

NPPF (2019) – the National Planning Policy Framework (2019)

NRBW – the Natural Resources Body for Wales

NSIPs – Nationally Significant Infrastructure Projects

PPG – the Planning Practice Guidance

PPW – Planning Policy Wales

SPPS – Strategic Planning Policy Statement for Wales (2015)

The Welsh Circular – Working Together for Wales: Policy Statement for the National Parks and National Park Authorities in Wales (2007)

WFD – The Water Framework Directive (2000/60/EC) as amended by Directives 2008/105/EC, 2013/39/EU and 2014/101/EU.

# CONTENTS

# CHAPTER ONE

# INTRODUCTION

*James Maurici QC and Nick Grant*

# 1. NATIONAL PARKS, AONBS AND THE BROADS: AN INTRODUCTION

1.1 We are extremely fortunate in this country to enjoy some truly magnificent landscapes, ranging from towering peaks to lowland fens. We are, rightly, proud of these landscapes, such that their protection, and our rights to roam in them, are of the utmost import.

1.2 The system that has developed for their protection depends on the designation of those landscapes as a National Park ("NP"), Area of Outstanding Natural Beauty ("AONB"), or as part of the Norfolk and Suffolk Broads. At present, approximately 24.5% of England is currently covered by NPs, the Broads, or AONBs.[1] In Wales, as Planning Policy Wales explains "...a quarter of the land area of Wales is designated as either a National Park or Area of National Outstanding Beauty (AONB)"[2]. It is beyond the scope of this book to consider the many local landscape designations that exist in Development Plans. Nor, as we are barristers qualified in England & Wales and Northern Ireland, does this book cover Scotland.

1.3 In the remainder of this chapter, we briefly outline the legislative history of NPs, AONBs and the Broads, looking at their statutory underpinning, government guidance, and potential for reform. We then examine, in detail, their role in the planning system (Chapters 2-3), before looking at the application of national policy and guidance (Chapter 4), wildlife and biodiversity issues (Chapter 5), and water issues (Chapter 6). We will conclude by looking at the various rights of way and access rights granted to members of the public (Chapters 7-8).

---

1 See *Landscapes Review: Final report – summary of findings* (25 September 2019) at https://www.gov.uk/government/publications/designated-landscapes-national-parks-and-aonbs-2018-review/landscapes-review-summary-of-findings accessed 26 May 2020.

2 See para. 6.32, and see further Chapter 4.

## National Parks, the Broads, and AONBs – a potted legislative history

National Parks

1.4 The first Freedom to Roam bill was introduced into parliament by James Bryce MP in 1884. It failed, but the campaign for the right for public access had begun. Over the following years, until 1914, similar bills were introduced and voted down, and regular petitions were presented to parliament. In 1931, the *Report of the National Park Committee* (1931) (Cmd 3851) recommended, among other things, setting up National Authorities for parks to ensure the preservation of natural beauty in the countryside. That was not, however, implemented, leading to further public pressure. In April 1945, Mr John Dower provided a report to the minister of town and country planning on NPs: *National parks in England and Wales* (1945) (Cmd 6628). That report provided the foundation for the detailed proposals subsequently prepared by the National Parks Committee, chaired by Sir Arthur Hobhouse. It reported in 1947 with the *Report of the National Parks Committee (England and Wales)* (1947) (Cmd 7121).

1.5 In 1949, Parliament enacted the National Parks and Access to the Countryside Act 1949 ("the 1949 Act"). This allowed for the creation of NPs. Over the following decade, ten NPs were designated. They, and their dates of confirmation, are: the Peak District (1951); Lake District (1951); Snowdonia (1951), Dartmoor (1951), Pembrokeshire Coast (1952), North York Moors (1952), Yorkshire Dales (1954), Exmoor (1954), Northumberland (1956), and the Brecon Beacons (1957).

1.6 In 1985, the Nature Conservation and Amenity Lands (Northern Ireland) Order 1985 ("the 1985 Order") was published. In 1989, the Nature Conservation and Amenity Lands (Amendment) (Northern Ireland) Order 1989/492 amended the 1985 Order, and established the Council for Nature Conservation and the Countryside. Articles 13 and 14 of the 1985 Order allow the Department of the Environment of Northern Ireland to designate areas as NPs. At the time of writing no such areas have been designated, although the Mourne Mountains is frequently suggested, and significant controversy surrounds the failure to so designate.

1.7 In 1995, following the delivery of the report *Fit for the Future (Report of the National Parks Review Panel* (1991), the Environment Act 1995 ("the EA 1995") updated the purposes of NPs, and made the National Park Authorities ("NPAs") independent bodies within local government.

1.8 In 2000, the National Parks (Scotland) Act 2000 created a similar scheme for National Parks in Scotland. Two have been designated –Loch Lomond & The Trossachs (2002) and the Cairngorms (2003).

1.9 Both the 1949 Act and the EA 1995 were subsequently amended by the Natural Environment and Rural Communities Act 2006 ("the NERC Act 2006").

1.10 The New Forest was confirmed as a NP in 2006, the South Downs in 2010.

1.11 National Parks England ("NPE") is an association of the National Parks in England plus the Broads.

## The Broads

1.12 The Broads comprise over 300 square kilometres of wetland landscapes in east Norfolk and Suffolk. In Howell v Secretary of State for Communities and Local Government [2014] EWHC 3627 (Admin), it was described by the Broads Authority as:

> *"the United Kingdom's largest protected wetland and boast[ing] a quarter of its rarest species. The broad, shallow lakes are man-made rather than natural. They began as pits dug for peat to provide fuel during medieval times. Over the centuries water levels rose, the peat diggings became flooded and by the 14th century*

*they were abandoned'. The special characteristics of the Broads, as summarised from the Broads Plan 2011, are the wide, open landscape, the winding waterways, the big skies, the abundance and diversity of nature, the sense of space, tranquillity and wildness, the local character of beautiful churches, windmills and quiet villages, and the opportunities for boating and sailing."* (at [37]).

1.13 The advent of the protection of the Broads is recounted in R (Harris) v Broads Authority [2017] 1 W.L.R. 567 at paras. 13-14. Very briefly, although listed as a potential NP in the Hobhouse report, designation did not proceed in the 1950s. Following a deterioration of the water quality within the broads in the 1970s, the Countryside Commission resolved in 1978 that the Broads merited the distinction of designation as a NP, but deferred designation to allow steps to be taken locally to establish an executive committee similar to the structures then in place for NPs. Following consultation, it was concluded that, because of particular issues concerning the waterways, a standard NP solution should not be adopted and, instead, a bespoke arrangement pursued. Although initially this took the form of a joint committee of local authorities, the water authority, harbour master and other interests, it was later thought necessary for a bespoke statutory arrangement. In 1988, Parliament enacted the Norfolk and Suffolk Broads Act 1988 ("the NSBA 1988"), giving the Broads similar status to the NPs. They were confirmed in 1989. Further powers with regard to the waterways known as the "navigation area" were provided by the Broads Authority Act 2009 ("BAA 2009").

## Areas of Outstanding National Beauty

1.14 The 1949 Act also, in section 87, allowed the Countryside Commission to designate areas outside of the NPs as AONBs if they were of "such outstanding natural beauty" that it was desirable. Thirty seven AONBs were designated in England between 1957 and 1995, and five in Wales between 1956 and 1985.[3] However, there were concerns that the standards of management between AONBs varied. In 1998, the Countryside Commission produced a report entitled *Protecting our Finest Countryside: Advice to Government* (CCP 532).[4] This contained a number of proposals for ensuring that AONBs were better and more consistently managed. This led to Part IV of the Countryside and Rights of Way Act 2000 ("the 2000 Act"), which currently governs AONBs. It, too, has been amended by the NERC Act 2006.

1.15 In Northern Ireland, section 14 of the 1985 Order allows the Department for the Environment to designate an area as an AONB.

1.16 The UK currently has 46 AONBs – 33 in England, four in Wales, one crossing the border between England and Wales, and eight in Northern Ireland. Occasionally, the government may decide to expand the area of an AONB. For example, on 07 July 2020 the Suffolk Coast and Heaths AONB was extended by c. 38km$^2$, to include areas such as the Stour Estuary.[5]

## 2 STATUTORY PROVISIONS: A BRIEF OUTLINE

### National Parks

#### The purpose of National Parks legislation

2.1 Provision for NPs was made by Part II of the 1949 Act. S. 4A of the 1949 Act provides that Part II also applies in Wales, with the

3 See the Explanatory Notes to the Countryside and Rights of Way Act 2000, paras. 251-55.

4 A digital copy of this is available on the website of the National Association for AONBs, at https://landscapesforlife.org.uk/application/files/6315/5552/1975/CCP-532.pdf (accessed 26 May 2020).

5 See the government announcement at https://www.gov.uk/government/news/boost-for-picturesque-landscapes-as-suffolk-coast-and-heaths-area-of-outstanding-natural-beauty-extended

modification that the functions conferred on Natural England in England are conferred on the Natural Resources Body for Wales ("NRBW") in Wales.

2.2 The purposes of that Part are outlined in section 5(1):

> *"(1) The provisions of this Part of this Act shall have effect for the purpose—*
> *(a) of conserving and enhancing the natural beauty, wildlife and cultural heritage of the areas specified in the next following subsection; and*
> *(b) of promoting opportunities for the understanding and enjoyment of the special qualities of those areas by the public."*

2.3 There are thus two statutory purposes for NPs: (i) conserving and enhancing natural beauty etc. and (ii) promoting opportunities for public access.

2.4 Sub-section 114(2) provides that the conservation of natural beauty of an area includes preservation of conservation of its flora, fauna, geological and physiographical features.

2.5 In Northern Ireland, the 1985 Order is in similar terms. Section 12 provides:

> *12.—(1) Where, in relation to an extensive area of countryside, the Department considers it desirable that measures be taken for the purposes of—*
> *(a) conserving or enhancing the natural beauty or amenities of that area;*
> *(b) conserving wildlife, historic objects or natural phenomena therein;*
> *(c) promoting the enjoyment by the public of the area; and*
> *(d) providing or maintaining public access to the area;*
> *the Department may by order designate the area as a National Park.*

## Designation of National Parks

2.6 Section 5 of the 1949 Act continues:

> *"(2) The said areas are those extensive tracts of country in England as to which it appears to Natural England that by reason of—*
> *(a) their natural beauty, and*
> *(b) the opportunities they afford for open-air recreation, having regard both to their character and to their position in relation to centres of population,*
> *it is especially desirable that the necessary measures shall be taken for the purposes mentioned in the last foregoing subsection.*
>
> *(2A) Natural England may–*
> *(a) when applying subsection (2)(a) in relation to an area, take into account its wildlife and cultural heritage, and*
> *(b) when applying subsection (2)(b) in relation to that area, take into account the extent to which it is possible to promote opportunities for the understanding and enjoyment of its special qualities by the public.*
>
> *(3) The said areas, as for the time being designated by order made by Natural England and submitted to and confirmed by the Minister, shall be as known as, and are hereinafter referred to as, National Parks."*

2.7 In determining what constitutes "Natural beauty", section 99 of the NERC Act 2006 provides:

> *"The fact that an area in England or Wales consists of or includes—*
> *(a) land used for agriculture or woodlands,*
> *(b) land used as a park, or*

*(c) any other area whose flora, fauna or physiographical features are partly the product of human intervention in the landscape,*
*does not prevent it from being treated, for the purposes of any enactment (whenever passed), as being an area of natural beauty (or of outstanding natural beauty)."*

2.8 Sections 59 (which inserted section 2A of the 1949 Act) and 99 of the NERC Act 2006 were intended to undo the effects of the High Court's decision in Meyrick Estate Management Ltd v Secretary of State for the Environment, Food and Rural Affairs [2005] EWHC 2618 (Admin) (affirmed on appeal [2007] EWCA Civ 53).[6] That case concerned the registration of the Hinton Estate as a NP under section 5(2). Sullivan J held at paras. 58-61, that, at the time it was enacted, "natural beauty" required "a high degree of 'relative naturalness'", such that well maintained historic parkland and well-ordered fields of dairy farms would be the "antithesis" of naturalness. It was not synonymous with "visual attractiveness" or "landscape quality". Accordingly, a broader range of factors, such as historical and cultural factors, could not be taken into account. He also held, at para. 82, that the opportunities afforded for recreation in section 2(b) did not equate with opportunities that *could be* afforded – so absent any track record of granting access, desire to do so, or prospect of the public being able to require access under other enactments, there were no more than vague aspirations under that section. An order could not be based on those.

2.9 For the purposes of sub-section 5(3), the procedure governing designation of an NP by Natural England or NRBW, and confirmation or variation of that Order by the Minister, is governed by section 7 and the First Schedule to the 1949 Act.

2.10 Section 6 of the National Parks and Access to the Countryside Act 1949 then places three distinct duties on Natural England and NRBW with regard to NPs. First, they must, from time to

6 See paragraphs 167 and 230 of the Explanatory Notes to the NERC Act 2006

time, consider whether to designate additional areas as NPs. Second, they must consider under both the 1949 Act and the Town and Country Planning Acts what action must be taken for the purposes outlined in section 5(1), and make recommendations to the Secretary of State, NPAs and local authorities. Third, they are placed under a number of duties to advise the Secretary of State or local planning authorities with regard to proposed developments and development plans in NPs.

2.11 In Northern Ireland, the equivalent provisions are much shorter. As outlined above at para. 2.5, if the Department for the Environment considers that designation is desirable for the purposes set out therein, it may by order designate the area. The Department is to be advised by the Council for Nature Conservation and the Countryside.

National Park authorities

2.12 Section 63 of the EA 1995 gives the Secretary of State power to establish, by order, a NPA in respect of any land designated as a NP. Section 64 gives him power to reconstitute Welsh National Park planning boards as NPAs. Section 63(7) and Schedule 7 make provision for, among other things, the membership of NPAs.[7]

2.13 The powers of NPAs are provided by sections 65-70 and Schedules 8-9 of the EA 1995. They are explored in more detail in Chapter 2 and so only outlined (very) broadly here. This

7 Broadly, paragraph 1 of Schedule 7 provides that a National Park authority shall consist of a specified number of local authority members, (in England) parish members appointed by the Secretary of State, and specified number of other members to be appointed by the Secretary of State. See the National Park Authorities (England) Order 2006/3165 and the National Park Authorities (England) Order 2015/770, the National Park Authorities (Wales) Order 1995/2803, the New Forest National Park Authority (Establishment) Order 2005/421 and the South Downs National Park Authority (Establishment) Order 2010/497. Most have been amended by various other statutory instruments.

includes consideration of the duty to have in place a National Park Management Plan: see section 66 of the EA 1995[8].

2.14 The purpose of establishing and providing powers to NP authorities is outlined by section 65(1) the EA 1995:

> *"(1) This Part so far as it relates to the establishment and functions of National Park authorities shall have effect for the purposes specified in section 5(1) of the National Parks and Access to the Countryside Act 1949 (purposes of conserving and enhancing the natural beauty, wildlife and cultural heritage of National Parks and of promoting opportunities for the understanding and enjoyment of the special qualities of those Parks by the public)."*

2.15 Section 11A(1) of the 1949 Act further provides:

> *"(1) A National Park authority, in pursuing in relation to the National Park the purposes specified in subsection (1) of section five of this Act, shall seek to foster the economic and social well-being of local communities within the National Park and shall for that purpose co-operate with local authorities and public bodies whose functions include the promotion of economic or social development within the area of the National Park."*

2.16 In R (Harris) v Broads Authority [2017] 1 W.L.R. 567, Holgate J said this subsection

> *"...imposes relatively broad duties, which are largely dependent upon the value judgments made by a National Park Authority from time to time. The subsection is directed at the promotion of broad objectives*

---

8 https://www.nationalparksengland.org.uk/national-park-management-plans

> *and securing co-operation between public bodies within that context..." (at [75]).*

2.17 A NPA's powers include the power to do anything which, in its opinion, is calculated to facilitate, or is conducive or incidental to, the accomplishment of the purposes outlined in section 5(1) of the 1949 Act and (in Wales) the carrying out of any functions conferred on it by any other statute (section 65(5)(a) and (b) of the EA 1995). In England, in place of the powers outlined in section 65(5)(b), general powers and their limitations are provided by Section 65A-D of the EA 1995. It is given authority to do anything it considers appropriate for the purposes of carrying out its functions or for purposes incidental to its functional purposes, anything it considers connected with those functions or incidences, or anything it could do in that capacity for a commercial purpose (see section 65A(1) the EA 1995). The Secretary of State may, however, make regulations restricting the exercise of those powers (sections 65C-D of the EA 1995). Supplemental and incidental powers are provided by Schedule 8 to the EA 1995. A NPA is also made the local planning authority in relation to the NP (see sections 67-69 EA 1995 and section 4A of the Town and Country Planning Act 1990 ("TCPA 1990")), must develop a National Park Management Plan (section 66 of the EA 1995) and is given further miscellaneous functions by section 70 and Schedule 9 to the EA 1995.

National Parks' role in the planning system

2.18 In contrast to the section 11A(1) duty imposed on NPAs, section 11A(2) of the 1949 Act then places a duty on relevant public authorities (widely defined by sub-sections 11A(3)-(6) to include ministers of the Crown, public bodies and statutory undertakers). Section 11A(2) provides:

> *"[i]n exercising or performing any functions in relation to, or so as to affect, land in a National Park, any relevant authority shall have regard to the purposes specified*

> *in subsection (1) of section five of this Act and, if it appears that there is a conflict between those purposes, shall attach greater weight to the purpose of conserving and enhancing the natural beauty, wildlife and cultural heritage of the area comprised in the National Park."*

2.19 The second part of this clause (prioritising the conservation and enhancement over public enjoyment) implements what is known as the Sandford Principle. It arose in a report of the National Park Policies Review Committee, chaired by Lord Sandford, in 1974, effectively to ensure that excessive enjoyment did not undermine the conservation of natural beauty. It has been considered briefly in R (Harris) at paras 85-87. In Stubbs (on behalf of Green Lanes Environmental Action Movement) v Lake District National Park Authority [2020] EWHC 2293 (Admin), Dove J held that the Sandford Principle and s. 11A(2) could only be invoked when the NPA considered, using its own judgment, that there was an irreconcilable conflict between the two purposes of NPs. He said:

> *" … the use of the word "conflict" in section 11A(2) is not to be understood as referring to any conflict or friction between the two purposes set out in section 5. Those purposes will very often be at odds with each other in the absence of any intervention to resolve them (such as the erosion caused to popular paths by walkers, cyclists or horse riders). Thus, something more than simply conflict which is not managed must arise for the provisions of section 11A(2) to be triggered. In truth, it does not appear that this proposition is controversial. Where the National Park Authority judges that the conflict can no longer be satisfactorily mediated through management or stewardship then, in circumstances where it is judged that both purposes cannot be accommodated and the National Park Authority concludes that it must make a choice, section 11A(2) makes clear that it is the first of the purposes which is to be afforded greater weight.*

*Whether this is described as a conflict which is acute, or unresolvable, or irreconcilable is a matter of semantics. However, each of these adjectives properly describes the point at which section 11A(2) comes into play, in order to resolve a conflict which cannot be properly accommodated through management measures when greater weight then has to attach in the decision-taking process to the first purpose of conserving and enhancing the natural beauty, wildlife and cultural heritage of the area comprised in the national park". (at [39])*

*"In my view Holgate J was correct [(in Harris)] when he observed that the provisions of section 11A(2) impose "relatively broad duties, which are largely dependent upon the value judgements made by a National Park Authority from time to time". It is clear that broad and often subjective judgements will need to be formed by a National Park Authority in relation to how the best interests of both of the purposes set out in section 5 are to be served by the decisions which it makes. In addition to these judgments, the question of whether or not there is a conflict which engages section 11A(2) is a further exercise of judgment in relation to the broad duties imposed on the National Park Authority. What is clear from the language of the statute, and the way in which section 5 and section 11A(2) of the 1949 Act interrelate, is that section 11A(2) arises in circumstances where the National Park Authority reaches the judgment that a conflict between the two purposes is such that it cannot be resolved or reconciled and the preference for the first statutory purpose under section 5 of the 1949 Act must arise. Section 11A(2) is a necessary means of breaking the deadlock where the interests of the two purposes cannot be mediated through a management or stewardship solution". (at [40])*

2.20 Some key points need elaboration. First, the duty applies where a relevant authority is exercising or performing any functions "in relation to, or so as to affect, land in a National Park". This is very widely drawn – we think deliberately so.

2.21 Second, "functions" as used in section 11A of the 1949 Act, includes both powers and duties. In Hazell v Hammersmith and Fulham LBC [1992] 2 AC 1, the House of Lords considered that term within the meaning of section 111 of the Local Government Act 1972. Lord Templeman said:

> *"'functions' embraces all the duties and powers of a local authority; the sum total of the activities Parliament has entrusted to it. Those activities are its functions" (at p. 29)*

2.22 Third, the duty is "to have regard to" the NP purposes. The effect of this is that in exercising or performing any such function the relevant authority is legally required to give consideration to the NP purposes. It is process rather than outcome oriented – it does not, for example, dictate that planning permission must be refused in a given case or that a plan must have any particular content. The Courts would generally expect that the relevant authorities should be able to clearly show how they considered the purposes of the NPs in their decision making.

2.23 Fourth, the weight to be given to such purposes, and the weight of those purposes against any countervailing considerations, is entirely a matter for the relevant authority, subject to the restraint that it cannot be "irrational" in the sense outlined in Associated Provincial Picture Houses Ltd v Wednesbury Corp [1948] 1 KB 233. In Tesco Stores Ltd v Secretary of State for the Environment [1995] 1 W.L.R. 759, Lord Hoffman said that, where a decision maker must have regard to a matter,

> *"it is at liberty (provided that it does not lapse into Wednesbury irrationality) to give them whatever weight the … authority thinks fit or no weight at all. The fact that*

*the law regards something as a material consideration therefore involves no view about the part, if any, which it should play in the decision-making process ...*" (at p.780)

2.24 Fifth, the purposes outlined in section 11A(2) are not exhaustive of all that a decision maker will need to consider. As Holgate J said in R (Harris):

> "*UK National Parks, unlike national parks in some other countries, are not publicly owned. Much of the land is privately owned and used, for example, for agriculture or forestry: see para 1.5 of the Sandford Report. Thus, section 11A(2) only requires a "relevant authority" to have regard to the twin purposes set out in section 5(1) of the 1949 Act. Moreover, those purposes are not exhaustive of all the considerations which will have to be taken into account when decisions are made on land use within a National Park, for example on farming practices or planning control decisions. The Sandford Principle in section 11A(2) only deals with the relationship between the "conservation" objective and the "public enjoyment" objective. It does not deal with all relevant considerations which may have to be taken into account in a planning decision, such as the need for development including housing and economic need.*" (at [86])

2.25 There is no clear equivalent of section 11A(2) in the 1985 Order for Northern Ireland. The closest is a much more general duty, not restricted to NPs or their aims, in Article 4:

> ***"Duty of public bodies***
>
> *4.—(1) In exercising functions relating to land under any statutory provision, public bodies shall have regard to the need to conserve the natural beauty and amenity of*

*the countryside and the need to protect (so far as reasonably practicable) flora, fauna and geological and physiographical features of the countryside from any harmful effects which might result from the exercise of such functions.*

*(2) In paragraph (1) the expression "public bodies" includes government departments, district councils and statutory undertakers, and any trustees, commissioners, board or other persons who, as a public body and not for their own profit, act under any statutory provision for the improvement of any place or the production or supply of any commodity or service."*

## The Broads

2.26 The full extent of the Broads is defined by section 2(3) NSBA 1988 as the area coloured pink on the deposited map, subject to any variations. The legislative scheme is similar to that for NPs, but with some key differences, outlined below.

### Broads Authorities

2.27 The Broads Authority is set up by sections 1-7 NSBA 1988. It is, in short, the body responsible for the conservation and promotion of the Broads, as well as navigation and planning functions within that area (R (Harris) at [15]). Section 1 NSBA 1988 establishes the Broads Authority and its constitution of members.

2.28 The Broads Authority's general duty is outlined by section 2(1):

*"(1) It shall be the general duty of the Authority to manage the Broads for the purposes of—*
*(a) conserving and enhancing the natural beauty, wildlife and cultural heritage of the Broads;*
*(b) promoting opportunities for the understanding and enjoyment of the special qualities of the Broads by the public; and*

> *(c) protecting the interests of navigation."*

2.29 The first two of these purposes mirror those for NPs, the third is bespoke to the Broads.

2.30 In discharging that duty, section 2(4) provides that it "shall have regard to"

> *"(a) the national importance of the Broads as an area of natural beauty and one which affords opportunities for open-air recreation;*
> *(b) the desirability of protecting the natural resources of the Broads from damage; and*
> *(c) the needs of agriculture and forestry and the economic and social interests of those who live or work in the Broads."*

2.31 This "general duty" is in different terms to the legislative scheme in the 1949 Act, where a NPA must simply "have regard to" the purposes outlined in section 5(1) of that Act. Moreover, there is no statutory scheme of priorities either between the purposes outlined in section 2(1) or the considerations in section 2(4). The Sandford Principle has not been incorporated. In practice, the weight to be given to each of the purposes in section 2(1) will depend on the circumstances under consideration (see R (Harris) at [17]-[19]).

2.32 As with NPAs, the Broads Authority is made the sole district planning authority with regard to the Broads (section 2(5) and Part 1 of Schedule 3 NSBA 1988), and granted a number of miscellaneous functions (section 2(6) and Part II of Schedule 3 NSBA 1988). It is also given power to, per section 2(7):

> *"[...] do anything which is necessary or expedient for the purpose of enabling it to carry out its functions, or for incidental purposes, including power—*
> *(a) to acquire, manage, reclaim and dispose of land or other property;*

*(b) to carry out any building or other operations; and*
*(c) to carry on any business or undertaking."*

2.33 Section 21 and Schedule 6 of the NSBA 1988 amend legislation to apply section 111 of the Local Government Act 1982 to the Broads Authority. That states:

> *"(1) Without prejudice to any powers exercisable apart from this section but subject to the provisions of this Act and any other enactment passed before or after this Act, a local authority shall have power to do any thing (whether or not involving the expenditure, borrowing or lending of money or the acquisition or disposal of any property or rights) which is calculated to facilitate, or is conducive or incidental to, the discharge of any of their functions."*

2.34 By section 6, it is given the power to create byelaws to secure that persons do not damage the land or unduly interfere with the enjoyment of land by others. By section 5, it is to the Broads Authority that persons must apply for consent if they wish to undertake a specified activity in specified land outlined an order made by the Secretary of State.

2.35 The Broads Authority, like NPAs, must prepare and review a Broads Plan setting out its policy with respect to the exercise of its functions (section 3). In addition, it must prepare, publish, and keep under review a map showing any areas within the Broads whose natural beauty is, in its opinion, particularly important to conserve (section 4).

2.36 The Broads authority is treated as being a NPA for certain statutory purposes, such as for the purposes of the Derelict Land Act 1982, or for the purposes of the making of grants and loans under section 44 of the Wildlife and Countryside Act 1981 (see paragraphs 31 and 43 of Schedule 3 to the 1988 Act).

Navigation Areas

2.37 Section 8 of the NSBA 1988 designates stretches of the various waterways within the Broads as "the navigation area." The Broads Authority must maintain the navigation area for the purposes of navigation, and take such steps to improve and develop it as it thinks fit. It must appoint a committee known as the Navigation Committee, which it must consult before undertaking certain actions which might "significantly affect the use or enjoyment" of the navigation area (section 9). It may make byelaws for the good management of the navigation area, and to conserve its natural beauty and amenities, and is given additional functions outlined by Part I of Schedule 5 (section 10). It may also set and charge tolls for vessels mooring, using, or navigating on waters in the navigation area and adjacent waters (section 13). Further powers are provided by the Broads Authority Act 2009.

Role in the planning system

2.38 Section 17A NSBA 1988 includes a duty on wider public authorities similar to that outlined by the first part of section 11A(2) of the 1949 Act. However, it includes a third additional objective and does not incorporate the Sandford principle. It provides

> *"(1) In exercising or performing any functions in relation to, or so as to affect, land in the Broads, a relevant authority shall have regard to the purposes of—*
> *(a) conserving and enhancing the natural beauty, wildlife and cultural heritage of the Broads;*
> *(b) promoting opportunities for the understanding and enjoyment of the special qualities of the Broads by the public; and*
> *(c) protecting the interests of navigation."*

2.39 When considering the purpose of conserving and enhancing the natural beauty of the Broads, it is relevant to consider the extent to which the land affected exhibits the characteristics of the

Broads landscape: Howell v Secretary of State for Communities and Local Government [2015] EWCA Civ 1189, [26].

**Areas of Outstanding Natural Beauty**

2.40 Section 82(1) and (2) of the Countryside and Rights of Way Act 2000 Act ("the 2000 Act") provides Natural England and NRBW with the power to designate, by order, areas of outstanding natural beauty. Section 82(1) provides:

> *"(1) Where it appears to Natural England that an area which is in England but not in a National Park is of such outstanding natural beauty that it is desirable that the provisions of this Part relating to areas designated under this section should apply to it, Natural England may, for the purpose of conserving and enhancing the natural beauty of the area, by order designate the area for the purposes of this Part as an area of outstanding natural beauty."*

2.41 The procedure for a designation order is outlined in section 83.

2.42 The functions and powers of local planning authorities who have AONBs within their area is provided for by section 84. Section 84(1)-(3) applies Natural England's and NRBW's obligation to consult on, among other things, development matters in relation to AONBs as they apply to NPs. Sub-section 85(4)-(6) then provide:

> *"(4) A local planning authority whose area consists of or includes the whole or any part of an area of outstanding natural beauty has power, subject to subsections (5) and (6), to take all such action as appears to them expedient for the accomplishment of the purpose of conserving and enhancing the natural beauty of the area of outstanding natural beauty or so much of it as is included in their area.*

*(5) Nothing in this Part is to be taken to limit the generality of subsection (4); but in so far as the provisions of this Part or of the 1949 Act confer specific powers falling within that subsection those powers are to be exercised in accordance with those provisions and subject to any limitations expressed or implied in them.*

*(6) Without prejudice to the powers conferred by this Part, subsection (4) has effect only for the purpose of removing any limitation imposed by law on the capacity of a local planning authority by virtue of its constitution, and does not authorise any act or omission on the part of such an authority which apart from that subsection would be actionable at the suit of any person on any ground other than such a limitation."*

2.43 In Northern Ireland, the power to designate an area as an AONB is contained in Article 14 of the 1985 Order:

*"14.—(1) Subject to paragraphs (2) to (4), where the Department considers an area (not being an area within a National Park) to be of such outstanding natural beauty that it is desirable that the provisions of this Article should apply to the area, the Department may make an order designating it as an area of outstanding natural beauty."*

Conservation boards

2.44 Section 86 of the 2000 Act allows the Secretary of State and National Assembly for Wales, by order, to establish conservation boards in relation to an AONB, and either transfer functions of local authorities to that board, or provide that the conservation board and local authority are to exercise those functions concurrently. This does not extend to functions of a local authority under Parts III (control over development), VII (enforcement) or XIII (application of the Act to crown land) of the Town and

Country Planning Act 1990, nor parts 2 (local development) or 6 (Wales) of the Planning and Compulsory Purchase Act 2004. The procedure and powers for the making of such an order by the Secretary of State or Welsh Ministers is contained in section 88. The constitution of such boards is outlined in Schedule 13, and the order may make further provision under section 86(5).

2.45 The general powers and purposes of conservation boards are outlined in section 87. Per section 87(1):

> *"(1) It is the duty of a conservation board, in the exercise of their functions, to have regard to—*
> *(a) the purpose of conserving and enhancing the natural beauty of the area of outstanding natural beauty, and*
> *(b) the purpose of increasing the understanding and enjoyment by the public of the special qualities of the area of outstanding natural beauty,*
> *but if it appears to the board that there is a conflict between those purposes, they are to attach greater weight to the purpose mentioned in paragraph (a).*
>
> *(2) A conservation board, while having regard to the purposes mentioned in subsection (1), shall seek to foster the economic and social well-being of local communities within the area of outstanding natural beauty and shall for that purpose co-operate with local authorities and public bodies whose functions include the promotion of economic or social development within the area of outstanding natural beauty."*

2.46 S. 87(1) appears to incorporate the Sandford Principle, but only in the duty placed on Conservation Boards.

2.47 Their powers include, per section 87(4):

> *"power to do anything which, in the opinion of the board, is calculated to facilitate, or is conducive or incidental to—*

> *(a) the accomplishment of the purposes mentioned in subsection (1), or*
> *(b) the carrying out of any functions conferred on it by virtue of any other provision of this Part or by virtue of any enactment not contained in this Part."*

2.48 This does not include acting contrary to any other enactment or raising money (section 87(5)).

2.49 Supplemental and incidental powers are provided in Schedule 14. The order under section 86(1) may make further provision with respect to the supplemental and incidental powers of the conservation board, or provide for any enactment relating to or limiting the supplemental or incidental powers or duties on local authorities to apply to the conservation boards.

2.50 Conservation boards must also prepare, publish and keep under review management plans: see sections 89-90.

2.51 There are only two established Conservation Boards: see the Chilterns Area of Outstanding Natural Beauty (Establishment of Conservation Board) Order 2004/1778 and the Cotswolds Area of Outstanding Natural Beauty (Establishment of Conservation Board) Order 2004/1777.

2.52 In Northern Ireland, the Department may (per Article 14(5) of the 1985 Order):

> *"(5) Subject to paragraph (6), the Department may, in relation to an area designated by order under paragraph (1), formulate proposals for—*
> *(a) conserving or enhancing the natural beauty or amenities of that area;*
> *(b) conserving wildlife, historic objects or natural phenomena within it;*
> *(c) promoting its enjoyment by the public;*
> *(d) providing or maintaining public access to it."*

2.53 As with NPs, the Department must consult with, among other bodies, the Council for Nature Conservation and the Countryside.

Role in planning

2.54 Section 85(1) of the 2000 Act imposes the following duty on public bodies:

> *"(1) In exercising or performing any functions in relation to, or so as to affect, land in an area of outstanding natural beauty, a relevant authority shall have regard to the purpose of conserving and enhancing the natural beauty of the area of outstanding natural beauty."*

2.55 This is similar to, yet different again from the general duty imposed on public bodies under both the 1949 Act and NSBA 1988. What the general authority is to "have regard to" is narrower than in either of the other acts – conserving and enhancing natural beauty rather than the dual purposes outlined in section 5(1) of the 1949 Act or triple purposes outlined in section 17A NSBA 1988. Moreover, like section 17A NSBA 1988 but unlike section 11A(2) of the 1949 Act, the Sandford Principle is not incorporated into the general duty on public bodies.

2.56 The duty on public bodies in the 1985 Order has already been outlined, above at para. 2.25.

## 3 PLANNING GUIDANCE

3.1 Against that statutory background, the Government has issued a number of planning guidance documents that bear on the question of how landscapes are to be taken into account in planning decisions. This guidance and its effects are explored in detail in Chapter 4.

## National Planning Policies

3.2 Of key importance is the Government's National Planning Policy Framework (2019) (the "NPPF (2019)"). It replaces a previous NPPF, published in 2012 (the "NPPF (2012)"). The NPPF sets out the Government's planning policy for England, and how it should be applied. It provides a framework for the development of local plans, and is a material consideration to be taken into account when a decision is to be made on applications for planning permission. The importance of NPs, AONBs and the Broads is repeatedly emphasised throughout the NPPF (2019). In very broad outline, there is, in the NPPF (2019), a general presumption in favour of sustainable development (see para. 11). This presumption may be disapplied, however, if certain policies for protecting important assets of particular importance provide a clear reason for doing so. Policies relating to the protection of NPs, AONBs and the Broads are such policies – see para. 11(d)(i)fn6. Those policies are contained in Chapter 15 of the NPPF (2019). Of key importance is para. 172, which states that "Great weight" should be given to conserving and enhancing the landscape and scenic beauty in NPs, the Broads and AONBs and limits the scale and extent of development in these areas. Furthermore, although government policy requires local planning authorities to support the development of entry-level sites for first time buyers, on land which is not already allocated for housing, these should not be permitted within NPs, AONBs, within the Broads (see para. 71(b) fn 34).

3.3 In Wales, the key document is Planning Policy Wales (Edition 10, December 2018) ("PPW"). The PPW is in different terms to the NPPF, and is explored in more detail below in Chapter 4. It discusses NPs and AONBs at paras. 6.3.5 to 6.3.10, again noting that "great weight" should be given to conserving and enhancing NPs and AONBs, and the special qualities of both. Again, development, and particularly major development, is restricted in these areas.

3.4 In Northern Ireland, the Strategic Planning Policy Statement for Northern Ireland (2015) ("SPPS") discusses AONBs in policy making at para 6.155. It states that Local Development Plans should:

> *" … identify areas which should be protected from minerals development because of their intrinsic landscape, amenity, scientific or heritage value (including natural, built and archaeological heritage). There should be a general presumption against minerals development in such areas. However, where a designated area such as an Area of Outstanding Natural Beauty (AONB) covers expansive tracts of land, the LDP should carefully consider the scope for some minerals development that avoids key sites and that would not unduly compromise the integrity of the area as a whole or threaten to undermine the rationale for the designation."*

3.5 Their role in decision taking is discussed at paras. 6.186-6.188:

> *"6.187 Development proposals in AONBs must be sensitive to the distinctive special character of the area and the quality of their landscape, heritage and wildlife, and be in the accordance with relevant plan policies.*
>
> *6.188 In assessing proposals, including cumulative impacts in such areas, account will also be taken of the Landscape Character Assessments and any other relevant guidance including AONB Management Plans and local design guides."*

3.6 Preceding the SPPS, and still in use, is *Planning Policy Statement 2: Natural Heritage* (2013). Policy NH6 relates to AONBs. It is explored more in Chapter 4.

## National Planning Practice Guidance

3.7 Supplementing the NPPF is further Planning Practice Guidance (the "PPG"), published online by the Government.[9] At the time of writing, advice on NPs, the Broads and AONBs is contained in the collection entitled Natural Environment, specifically paragraphs 38-43.[10] This highlights, again, the importance of protecting NPs, the Broads, and AONBs. Paragraphs 041 and 042, for example, note that the restriction of development in these areas may mean it is not possible to meet the objectively assessed needs for housing in a given area, or that development which could affect long views both into and out of those areas needs particularly sensitive handling. The PPG also notes that the management plans prepared in each of these areas may contain relevant information or material considerations.

3.8 In Wales, the Welsh Government publishes Planning Policy and Guidance for Professionals ("PPGP"), also online.[11]

## Other Policy Statements

3.9 In 2010, Defra published *English National Parks and the Broads: UK Government Vision and Circular 2010*[12] (the "NP Circular") to provide policy guidance on English NPs and the Broads. Although, as we have seen, NPs and the Broads are established under two separate Acts of Parliament, Defra considered that the two were so similar that the Circular could be applied to both (see para. 3). The Circular sets out, among other things, a "vision for the English National parks and the Broads for 2030". This is intended to guide the long-term planning and strategic decision-making of the Authorities, and should be used for other public

---

9 https://www.gov.uk/government/collections/planning-practice-guidance

10 https://www.gov.uk/guidance/natural-environment

11 https://gov.wales/planning-policy-and-guidance-for-professionals

12 https://assets.publishing.service.gov.uk/government/uploads/system/uploads/attachment_data/file/221086/pb13387-vision-circular2010.pdf

bodies with a statutory interest under section 11A of the 1949 Act and section 17A of the 1988 Act to inform their decisions on how to meet their statutory duty to "have regard to" Park purposes (see para. 10 of the Circular). Although the Circular predates the NPPF, the NPPG still refers readers to it.[13] There is no equivalent circular for AONBs, but the NPPG directs readers to information published by Natural England on the government website.[14]

3.10 In Wales, a similar circular was published in 2007. However, that has likely been overtaken by the Welsh Government's more recent publication *Valued and Resilient: The Welsh Government's Priorities for Areas of Outstanding Natural Beauty and National Parks* (July 2018).[15] – see below.

## 4 THE FUTURE OF NATIONAL PARKS AND AONBS

4.1 Major reviews of NPs have been undertaken in recent years in both England and Wales. In Northern Ireland, the last review appears to have been around 2009-2010.

4.2 In Wales Prof. Terry Marsden, delivered *National Landscapes: Realising their Potential (Final Report)* in July 2015.[16] The Welsh Government has built on the proposals contained therein, and now published *Valued and Resilient.* This outlines four goals for AONBs and NPs in Wales – that they be valued places engaging a diverse cross section of welsh society, form resilient environments enhancing the value of nature and reversing biodiversity decline, that the support resilient communities, and that AONB

---

13 NPPG Paragraph: 038 Reference ID: 8-038-20190721

14 Ibid, redirecting readers to https://www.gov.uk/guidance/areas-of-outstanding-natural-beauty-aonbs-designation-and-management

15 https://gov.wales/sites/default/files/publications/2019-04/areas-outstanding-natural-beauty-national-parks-2018-report%20.pdf

16 https://gov.wales/sites/default/files/publications/2019-05/areas-outstanding-natural-beauty-national-parks-2015-report.pdf

partnerships and NPAs adopt more resilient ways of working, working more closely with one another.

4.3 In England, the Government set out in its policy paper *A Green Future: Our 25 Year Plan to Improve the Environment* (2018)[17] and intention to commission an independent Hobhouse style review of NPs, the Broads and AONBs. This was commissioned in May 2018. It was led by Julian Glover, and submitted its final report on 21 September 2019: *Landscapes Review (Final Report)* (Sept 2019) (the "Glover Review").[18]

4.4 The Glover Review has put together 27 proposals, broken down into five categories for reform of NPs, the Broads and AONBs. First, in light of fragmented yet alarming reports on the state of nature in the NPs and AONBs, the review recommends:

> *"Proposal 1: National landscapes should have a renewed mission to recover and enhance nature, and be supported and held to account for delivery by a new National Landscapes Service*
> *Proposal 2: The state of nature and natural capital in our national landscapes should be regularly and robustly assessed, informing the priorities for action*
> *Proposal 3: Strengthened Management Plans should set clear priorities and actions for nature recovery including, but not limited to, wilder areas and the response to climate change (notably tree planting and peatland restoration). Their implementation must be backed up by stronger status in law*

17 Available at https://assets.publishing.service.gov.uk/government/uploads/system/uploads/attachment_data/file/693158/25-year-environment-plan.pdf accessed 26 May 2020

18 Available at https://assets.publishing.service.gov.uk/government/uploads/system/uploads/attachment_data/file/833726/landscapes-review-final-report.pdf accessed 26 May 2020

> *Proposal 4: National landscapes should form the backbone of Nature Recovery Networks – joining things up within and beyond their boundaries*
> *Proposal 5: A central place for national landscapes in new Environmental Land Management Schemes*
> *Proposal 6: A strengthened place for national landscapes in the planning system with AONBs given statutory consultee status, encouragement to develop local plans and changes to the National Planning Policy Framework"*

4.5 At the time of writing, sections 95-99 Environment Bill 2020 include the requirement for the preparation of local nature recovery strategies for England. These will have to be prepared by, among others, a NPA and the Broads authority.

4.6 Second, the review states that NPs were created to, in part, provide a healing space for those who had given up so much during the second world war. They have not, however, reflected the changing and more diverse society that we now have. To ensure that landscapes of such import fulfil their original mission of providing opportunities for enjoyment and spiritual refreshment, the review recommends

> *"Proposal 7: A stronger mission to connect all people with our national landscapes, supported and held to account by the new National Landscapes Service*
> *Proposal 8: A night under the stars in a national landscape for every child*
> *Proposal 9: New long term programmes to increase the ethnic diversity of visitors*
> *Proposal 10: Landscapes that cater for and improve the nation's health and wellbeing*
> *Proposal 11: Expanding volunteering in our national landscapes*
> *Proposal 12: Better information and signs to guide visitors*

> *Proposal 13: A ranger service in all our national landscapes, part of a national family*
> *Proposal 14: National landscapes supported to become leaders in sustainable tourism*
> *Proposal 15: Joining up with others to make the most of what we have, and bringing National Trails into the national landscapes family*
> *Proposal 16: Consider expanding open access rights in national landscapes"*

4.7 Third, the review considers that the landscapes system works best when it works with people. A lived in village with an active school and working people is better than a sterile place full of "shuttered homes, empty pubs and derelict shops". Accordingly, the review recommends

> *"Proposal 17: National landscapes working for vibrant communities*
> *Proposal 18: A new National Landscapes Housing Association to build affordable homes*
> *Proposal 19: A new approach to coordinating public transport piloted in the Lake District, and new, more sustainable ways of accessing national landscapes"*

4.8 Fourth, the review considers there is a case for several larger AONBs to take on NP candidate status, as well as for a new AONB. It therefore recommends:

> *"Proposal 20: New designated landscapes and a new National Forest*
> *Proposal 21: Welcoming new landscape approaches in cities and the coast, and a city park competition*
> *Proposal 22: A better designations process"*

4.9 Finally, the review considers that for landscapes to focus on enhancing natural beauty, supporting communities and visitors, they will need to change and work together. It therefore recommends:

> *"Proposal 23: Stronger purposes in law for our national landscapes*
> *Proposal 24: AONBs strengthened with new purposes, powers and resources, renamed as National Landscapes*
> *Proposal 25: A new National Landscapes Service bringing our 44 national landscapes together to achieve more than the sum of their parts*
> *Proposal 26: Reformed governance to inspire and secure ambition in our national landscapes and better reflect society*
> *Proposal 27: A new financial model – more money, more secure, more enterprising"*

## 5 PLANNING FOR THE FUTURE

5.1 In August 2020 the Government published its White Paper *Planning for the Future.*

5.2 NPs and AONBs do not feature heavily.

5.3 In terms of NPs there are these two mentions:

> *"2.25. It is proposed that the standard method would be a means of distributing the national housebuilding target of 300,000 new homes annually, and one million homes by the end of the Parliament, having regard to:*
> *• the extent of land constraints in an area to ensure that the requirement figure takes into account the practical limitations that some areas might face, including the presence of designated areas of environmental and heritage value, the Green Belt and flood risk. For example, areas in National Parks are highly desirable and housing supply has not kept up with demand; however, the whole purpose of National Parks would be undermined by multiple large scale housing developments so a standard method should factor this in …*

> *EFFECTIVE STEWARDSHIP AND ENHANCEMENT OF OUR NATURAL AND HISTORIC ENVIRONMENT*
> *3.22. The reformed planning system will continue to protect the places of environmental and cultural value which matter to us. Plans will still play a vital role in identifying not just areas of defined national and international importance (such as National Parks and Sites of Special Scientific Interest), but also those which are valued and defined locally ... "*

5.4 For AONBs the main mention is para. 2.8 where in setting out the proposals for all land to carry one of three designations, in relation to the third it is said:

> *"Areas that are Protected – this would include sites and areas which, as a result of their particular environmental and/or cultural characteristics, would justify more stringent development controls to ensure sustainability. This would include areas such as Green Belt, Areas of Outstanding Natural Beauty (AONBs), Conservation Areas, Local Wildlife Sites, areas of significant flood risk and important areas of green space. At a smaller scale it can continue to include gardens in line with existing policy in the National Planning Policy Framework. It would also include areas of open countryside outside of land in Growth or Renewal areas. Some areas would be defined nationally, others locally on the basis of national policy, but all would be annotated in Local Plan maps and clearly signpost the relevant development restrictions defined in the National Planning Policy Framework."*

5.5 NPs would presumably also be included in this category. So it seems that, however radical the changes elsewhere, the changes for land in NPs and AONBs is more limited. What the White Paper does not address, in proposing this three category zoning, is how to deal with land outside NPs, the Broads and AONBs but which development of might adversely affect the visual amenities of these designations. In the US where they have a zoning system protective zones have been introduced around National Parks.

# CHAPTER TWO

# THE ROLE OF NATIONAL PARK AUTHORITIES AND THE BROADS AUTHORITY IN THE PLANNING SYSTEM

*Matthew Dale-Harris and James Neill*

## 1 *STATUS OF THE NATIONAL PARK AND BROADS AUTHORITIES*

1.1 As explored in the previous chapter, the power to establish the modern National Park authorities ("NPAs") in England was conferred on the Secretary of State by section 63 of the EA 1995 in relation to England. The equivalent power for Wales is found in section 64.

1.2 These powers were first exercised in the National Park Authorities (England) Order 1996/1243 ("the 1996 Order") and National Park Authorities (Wales) Order 1995/2803 ("the 1995 Order"). These Orders established NPAs in respect of each of the NPs which had been previously been designated, seven in England and two in Wales.[1] The 1996 Order was later repealed and replaced by the National Park Authorities (England) Order 2015/770 ("the 2015 Order"). The various orders also provided for the replacement of the former local authority management arrange-

1 In England, article 3 of the 1996 Order provided that there shall be established for each NP an NPA "*to be known by the name of that National Park with the addition of the words "National Park Authority"*. In Wales, paragraph 1 of Schedule 1 to the 1995 Order specifies the names of each of the three NPAs in English and in Welsh.

ments[2] with the result that each of the pre-existing NPs in England[3] and Wales[4] now have NPAs.

1.3 For new national parks, the practice of the Secretary of State has been to establish new NPAs by specific order and the New Forest NPA and South Downs NPA were created by the New Forest National Park Authority (Establishment) Order 2005/421 and South Downs National Park Authority (Establishment) Order 2010/497 respectively.

1.4 National park boundaries are varied from time to time. Where this occurs the area for which the relevant NPA has competence is deemed to be the area as varied: section (3) of the Environment Act 1995.

1.5 The Broads Authority was set up by sections 1-7 of the NSBA 1988 and came into being on 6 June 1988. It is a body corporate which performs the functions conferred by that Act and the BAA

---

2 Prior to the EA 1995, for national parks in England planning functions were dealt with by joint or special planning boards under the LGA 1972 and TCPA 1990. In Wales, planning functions were exercised by National Park planning boards.

3 Under the National Park Authorities (England) Order 1996 (SI 1996/1243), the two special Planning Boards which had been established under section 2 were wound up, with effect from April 1, 1997, and seven National Park authorities were established in England, assuming full responsibilities from the same date. The Authorities are for the National Parks of Dartmoor, Exmoor, Lake District, Northumberland, North York Moors, Peak District and the Yorkshire Dales. The New Forest National Park Authority was established on 1 April 1995 and the South Downs National Park Authority was established on 1 April 2011. The National Park Authorities (England) Order 2015 (SI 2015/770) revoked and replaced the National Park Authorities (England) Order 1996, together with its three amending instruments, with effect from 1 July 2015. It continues provision relating to the National Park authorities for National Parks in England established under the 1996 Order.

4 Under the National Park Authorities (Wales) Order 1995 (SI 1995/2803), new National Park authorities were established for the three existing National Parks in Wales, the Brecon Beacons National Park, the Pembrokeshire Coast National Park and the Snowdonia National Park.

2009. For many purposes, the Broads Authority is treated as a NPA.

## 2 *CONSTITUTION OF NPAS AND THE BROADS AUTHORITY*

2.1 Like local authorities, the NPAs and Broads Authority are each the creatures of statute and their status and constitution is defined in the relevant legislation.

2.2 For NPAs, the central provisions are to be found in Schedule 7 of the EA 1995, which is given effect by section 63(5) of the same Act.

2.3 The membership of NPAs is quite different to that of other planning authorities. Members of NPAs (and of the Broads Authority) are not elected but appointed: each NPA is a body corporate consisting of a specified number of members of different types. The total number and number of particular types of members varies from authority to authority, to reflect political and geographical considerations. They are set out in Schedule 1 of the National Parks Authorities (England) Order 2015/770 and the National Park Authorities (Wales) Order 1995/2803.

2.4 There are three types of member, one of which is only exists in the English NPAs:

a) In Wales and England, there are local authority members and other members appointed by the Secretary of State.

b) In England, there are also parish members.

2.5 The rules for each type of member are as follows

a) Local authority members, who must be members of the principal councils for the areas comprised in the NP, are appointed by those councils (paragraph 2 of Schedule

7). The appointments are subject to the requirement to take account of political balance under the Local Government and Housing Act 1989.

b) Other members are appointed in England by the Secretary of State after consultation with Natural England and in Wales by the Welsh Government after consultation with Natural Resources Wales (paragraph 4 of Schedule 7).

c) Parish members in England must be members of parish councils for parishes wholly or partly within the NP, or the chairman of a parish meeting for a parish which does not have a separate parish council (paragraph 3 of Schedule 7).

2.6 Schedule 7 makes further provision for the organisation and administration of NPAs, which is in general outside the scope of this work. Further supplementary provisions of specific relevance to NPAs are also contained in Schedules 2 and 3 of National Parks Authorities (England) Order 2015/770 and Schedules 3 to 5 of the National Park Authorities (Wales) Order 1995/2803.

**The Broads Authority**

2.7 The Broads Authority consists of nine members appointed by the various local authorities in Norfolk and Suffolk, ten members appointed by the Secretary of State, and two members appointed by the Broads Authority itself from those members of the navigation committee established under section 9 of the NSBA 1988 who are not already members.

2.8 Provision is made as to administration and functioning of the Broads Authority by Schedule 1 of the NSBA 1988. Notably, the Broads Authority may not appoint a chief officer without first consulting Natural England. Under sections 27 and 28 of the Localism Act 2011, the Broads Authority is under a duty to adopt a code of conduct and has done so.

## 3 NPAS AND THE BROADS AUTHORITY AS LOCAL PLANNING AUTHORITIES

3.1 Where an NPA has been established, it becomes the sole local planning authority for the area of the NP and has a full range of local planning functions and powers including in relation to minerals and waste planning. This is primarily established by section 4A into the TCPA 1990. Subsections 4A(2)-(3) provide that:

> *"(2) Subject to subsections (4) and (5) below, the National Park authority for the Park shall be the sole local planning authority for the area of the Park and, accordingly—*
>
> > *(a) functions conferred by or under the planning Acts on a planning authority of any description (including the functions of a mineral planning authority under those Acts and under the Planning and Compensation Act 1991) shall, in relation to the Park, be functions of the National Park authority, and not of any other authority; and*
> >
> > *(b) so much of the area of any other authority as is included in the Park shall be treated as excluded from any area for which that other authority is a planning authority of any description.*
>
> *(3) For the purposes of subsection (2) above functions under the planning Acts which (apart from this section) are conferred—*
>
> > *(a) in relation to some areas on the county or district planning authorities for those areas, and*
> >
> > *(b) in relation to other areas on the councils for those areas,*
>
> *shall be treated, in relation to those other areas, as conferred on each of those councils as the local planning authority for their area."*

3.2 The only exceptions are those powers under the TCPA 1990 which relate to tree protection and the proper maintenance of land. These are exercisable concurrently with the district council for an area where there is a district council: see subsection 4A(4):

> *"(4) The functions of a local planning authority by virtue of sections 198 to 201, 206 to 209 and 211 to 215, so far as they are functions of a National Park authority by virtue of this section, shall be exercisable as respects any area which is or is included in an area for which there is a district council, concurrently with the National Park authority, by that council."*

3.3 In contrast to the NPAs, the Broads Authority is only treated as the local planning authority for certain prescribed provisions – albeit that those provisions include almost all applicable powers under the TCPA 1990. Like NPAs, the majority of powers are solely exercisable by the Broads Authority (see powers listed in section 5(3) of the TCPA 1990) but for some powers in relation to trees and highways extinguishment orders it is only a local planning authority (see section 5(2) of the TCPA 1990).

3.4 In carrying out their statutory functions as local planning authorities, NPAs are subject to the same duties and have the same powers as other types of authority. However, they also subject to their overarching duties to pursue the purposes of conserving and enhancing the natural beauty, wildlife and cultural heritage of an area and of promoting opportunities for the understanding and enjoyment of the special qualities of the area: section 5(1) of the 1949 Act.[5] In doing so they must seek to foster the economic and social well-being of local communities within the national park, and must co-operate with local authorities and public bodies whose functions include the promotion of economic or social development within the area of the national park: section 11A of the 1949 Act, see again further Chapter 1.

---

5 See further Chapter 1 for a detailed discussion of these statutory duties.

3.5 This is perhaps of particular importance in relation to plan-making, where the test of soundness will include assessment of whether of development plan documents provide an appropriate context for the achievement of the national park purposes (this is discussed in section 6 below).

3.6 At the development control level, when determining whether to grant planning permission, the fact that development is in an AONB was confirmed by the Supreme Court in R (CPRE Kent) v Dover District Council [2018] 1 WLR 108 as one of the factors that can trigger the common law duty on LPAs to provide reasons. The Supreme Court affirmed the reasoning of Laws LJ in the Court of Appeal when he referred to three particular factors as calling for clear reasons in that case, including the "pressing nature" of the AONB policy as expressed in the NPPF which was described as conferring the "highest status of protection".[6] Thus LPAs (including NPAs) are likely to be held to a higher standard in respect of the provision of reasons for granting planning permission in AONBs.

3.7 The range of permitted development under the Town and Country Planning (General Permitted Development) (England) Order 2015 (SI 2015/596) ("GPDO") is restricted in NPs and the Broads. All land within them is "art.2(3) land" within Sch.1 to the Order, and reduced development tolerances are applied to it in Sch.2, in the following cases:

a) Part 1 (householder development): Classes A; AA; B; E; G; H and E.1 (f);

b) Part 3 (changes of use): Class J; JA; M; Q

c) Part 4 (temporary buildings and changes of use): Class E

d) Part 7 (non-domestic extensions, alterations etc): Class A; C; D; F; H; L

e) Part 9 (development relating to roads): Class D;

---

6 See the judgment of Lord Carnwath at [19] and [69].

f) Part 14 (renewable energy): Class H; I; J; K; N; O

g) Part 15 (power related development): Class B

h) Part 16 (communications): Class A; B; C

i) Part 19 (): Class B; T

j) Part 20 (construction of new dwellinghouse): Classes ZA; A; AA; AB; AC; AD;

3.8 Moreover, NP and Broads land is also article 2(4) land, which means that rights to undertake certain types of agricultural and forestry development under Part 6 of Schedule 2 to the GPDO are subject to a requirement of prior notification. The NPAs are entitled to insist that their prior approval be obtained to the siting and means of construction of any proposed private way, or the siting, design and external appearance of proposed buildings.

## 4 RELATIONSHIP OF NPAS TO OTHER LPAS

4.1 The designation of land as a NP or establishment of an NPA does not prevent that land from falling within areas of other local authorities and in practice there is a need for regular of collaboration and coordination – something which is in practice facilitated by the existence of the appointed local authority members. This is formally achieved in relation to development control decisions by the obligation to consult with the district council which would have been the local planning authority but for the establishment of the NPA in relation to applications for planning permission: see paragraph 4(2) of Schedule 1 of the TCPA 1990.

4.2 Consultation with the district councils will also be necessary in the context of plan-making, whether pursuant to the duty to co-operate or otherwise.

4.3 In relation to applications on land partly within and partly outside a NP there was, for a time, a degree of debate as to whether the whole application fell to be determined by the NPA. This was resolved by the High Court in R. v Northumberland National Park Authority ex p. Secretary of State for Defence (Moses J, (1999) 77 P. & C.R. 120. There, the Court was asked to declare which body was the local planning authority for the purposes of development on land partly inside and partly outside a NP. The court held that, reading section 4A(2) together with Schedule 1, it was the county council rather than the NPA which had the responsibility for the land outside of the NP. The NPA had powers in relation to land within the Park, but no powers outside it. By virtue of Sch.1, para.3(2), where land outside the Park was subject to a planning application which straddled a Park boundary, it was a county matter and was to be dealt with by the county planning authority.

4.4 While most NPAs have full provisioned planning teams which deal with the range of planning functions across the NP, an exception has emerged in respect of the South Downs National Park. The South Downs NP, which follows the ridge of a line of hills some 100 miles long, is unusual in that it overlaps with the areas of ten different LPAs.

4.5 To address that logistical challenge, the South Downs NPA has, since its establishment, operated via an agency agreement relating to the provision of planning services under section 101 of the Local Government Act 1972. This in effect creates a two-track system for development control matters whereby SDNPA Planning Officers deal with all planning matters in the following Local Authority areas directly:

a) Arun District Council

b) Adur & Worthing District Council

c) Brighton & Hove City Council

d) Mid-Sussex District Council

e) Wealden District Council

4.6 As well as minerals and waste planning issues for Hampshire, East Sussex & West Sussex county councils.

4.7 However, for applications within the areas of the five "host" authorities below, all planning questions, advice and applications are dealt with by the officers of those authorities on behalf of the SDNPA:

a) Chichester District Council

b) East Hampshire District Council

c) Horsham District Council

d) Lewes & Eastbourne District Council

e) Winchester City Council

## 5 NPAS AND EIA

5.1 Land within an NP or the Broads is a "sensitive area" under regulation 2 of the Town and Country Planning (Environmental Impact Assessment) (England) Regulations 2017 ("the EIA Regulations 2017") such that any development which falls within the first column of Schedule 2 and of which part is to be carried within the NP/Broads (other than exempt development in respect of which the Secretary of State has made a direction) is "Schedule 2 development" and must be screened before permission is granted: none of the normal thresholds are applicable.

## 6 NPAS AND PLAN-MAKING

6.1 NPAs like any other local planning authority have duties under section 19 of the 2004 Act to prepare development plans setting out, amongst other matters, the strategic priorities for the development and use of land in the authority's area.

6.2 A development plan promoted by an NPA, like all other local plans, has to meet the test of soundness set out in section 20(5) of the 2004 Act. That test requires plans to be positively prepared, justified, effective and consistent with national policy (as set out in paragraph 35 of the NPPF). However, in the case of NPAs, the function of plan-making differs to LPAs in that section 11A(2) provides that in exercising or performing any functions in relation to a NP a relevant authority shall have regard to purposes in section 5(1) (these are discussed in more detail above in Chapter 1). A relevant authority includes both an NPA and an Inspector appointed by the Secretary of State to examine any development plan document.

6.3 Section 5(1) and 11A(1) of the 1949 Act do not dictate the result of the exercise or performance of any functions including plan-making functions. The duty imposed by the statute under section 11A means that a NPA is to have regard to its statutory purposes when preparing and promoting a local plan. The statutory purposes are therefore material considerations to which regard must be had when an NPA is preparing a local plan. This is consistent with the NPPF which says that "great weight" must be given to conserving and enhancing landscape and scenic beauty in NPs.

6.4 The plans produce by the NPAs as planning authorities also have to interact with the management plans which are required to be produced under section 66 of the EA 1995. The purpose of those plans is to formulate a policy for the management of the Park and for carrying out the authority's functions in relation to the Park. Any proposal to publish, adopt or review a management plan must be notified to every principal council in the area, together with Natural England and, for Wales, the Natural Resources Body for Wales and their observations taken into account.

6.5 The South Downs Local Plan adopted in July 2019 must be the largest area of England ever covered by a Local Plan.

## 7 NPAS ROLE AS A CONSULTEE TO APPLICATIONS OUTSIDE BUT AFFECTING NPS

7.1 All local planning authorities are required by arts 18 and 19 of the Town and Country Planning (Development Management Procedure) (England) Order 2015 (SI 2015/595) (for England) and the Town and Country Planning (Development Management Procedure) (Wales) Order 2012 (SI 2012/801) (for Wales) and to consult with the NPA concerned before granting planning permission for any development likely to affect land in a National Park.

## 8 NPAS ROLE UNDER THE 2008 ACT

8.1 NPAs have a consultative role under the 2008 Act in relation to both national policy statements and nationally significant infrastructure projects ("NSIPs").

8.2 Under section 7 of the 2008 Act the Secretary of State must carry out such consultation and arrange for such publicity in relation to a draft national policy statement as he thinks appropriate. In deciding

8.3 They are also mandatory consultees on applications for development consent.

a) They must be consulted prior to the application under section 42 of the 2008 Act (read with section 43)

b) They must be given notice of the application once made (sections 56(2)(b) and section 56A of the 2008 Act)

c) They must be invited to the preliminary meeting by the Examining Authority under section 88(3) of the 2008 Act.

8.4 Those promoting NSIPs need to ensure they consult properly even at the early stages of a scheme. In 2018 the South Downs National Park Authority commenced judicial review proceedings to challenge Highways England's decision to select a modified version of option 5a as the preferred route for the A27 Arundel scheme. The authority argued Highways England had not followed the correct procedure in its consultation, which has to set out to the same level of detail for all of the options inside and outside the national park. In commencing the proceedings the then chair of the authority said: "We are not commencing proceedings for a judicial review lightly but we believe that Highways England have not followed the correct procedure, which was to set out, to the same level of detail, all of the options inside and outside the National Park. This led to them discounting options outside of the National Park too early in the process, and they have not provided any detail on mitigation and compensation for any of the routes. We want to work with Highways England so that they can find a solution to the traffic issues at Arundel that also protects the National Park for future generations, including having discussions around mitigation and compensation measures." The proceedings were withdrawn later than year when the agency announced it will be holding a new public consultation in the spring as 'important new information' about each of the options had become available.[7]

7 See https://www.littlehamptongazette.co.uk/news/politics/south-downs-withdraws-legal-challenge-highways-englands-a27-arundel-decision-224074.

# CHAPTER THREE

# AREAS OF OUTSTANDING NATURAL BEAUTY AND THE PLANNING SYSTEM

*Kate Olley and Matthew Dale-Harris*

## *1. AONBS AND THEIR CREATION*

1.1 Natural England has the power, by order, to designate an area in England as an area of outstanding natural beauty. The decision to designate will depend on Natural England's judgement. It has a discretion as to whether to assess and designate an area as an AONB. Such an area cannot be part of an area which is already in a National Park. The power is provided by section 82 of the Countryside and Rights of Way Act 2000 ("the 2000 Act"), within Part IV of the Act, entitled 'Areas of Outstanding Natural Beauty'.

1.2 The purpose of the order is to protect the land in order to conserve and enhance its natural beauty. Unlike National Parks, AONBs are not created specifically to provide opportunities for recreation. The conservation of the natural beauty of an area includes (s92(2) of the 2000 Act) a reference to the conservation of its flora, fauna and geological and physiographical features

1.3 Section 82 of the 2000 Act (entitled 'Designation of areas') provides:

> "*(1) Where it appears to Natural England that an area which is in England but not in a National Park is of such outstanding natural beauty that it is desirable that the provisions of this Part relating to areas designated under this section should apply to it, Natural England may, for the purpose of conserving and enhancing the natural beauty of the area, by order designate the area for the purposes of this Part as an area of outstanding natural beauty.*"

1.4 An identical provision in section 82(2) provides the same power to the Natural Resources Body for Wales ("NRBW").

1.5 In Northern Ireland the Northern Ireland Environment Agency ("NIEA") is responsible for the designation of AONBs, under the Amenity Lands Act (Northern Ireland) 1965 and the Nature

Conservation and Amenity Lands (Northern Ireland) Order 1985. Article 14 of the 1985 Order provides:

> "*(1) Subject to paragraphs (2) to (4), where the Department considers an area (not being an area within a National Park) to be of such outstanding natural beauty that it is desirable that the provisions of this Article should apply to the area, the Department may make an order designating it as an area of outstanding natural beauty.*"

1.6 There are currently 46 AONBs in the UK, including four wholly in Wales[1], 34 in England[2], one that lies on the border of England and Wales[3], and eight in Northern Ireland[4].

1.7 In relation to a proposal for designation, Natural England will take into account whether the evidence suggests that the land might need the natural beauty criterion and whether there is agreement from the local authority that a designation is appropriate.

1.8 The natural beauty criterion may be met by a combination of factors[5], including:

- Landscape quality- whether natural or manmade

1 Anglesey, Clwydian Range & Dee Valley, Gower, Llyn.

2 Arnside & Silverdale, Blackdown Hills, Cannock Chase, Chichester Harbour, Chilterns, Cornwall, Cotswolds, Cranborne Chase, Dedham Vale, Dorset, East Devon, Forest of Bowland, High Weald, Howardian Hills, Isle of Wight, Isles of Scilly, Kent Downs, Lincolnshire Woods, Malvern Hills, Mendip Hills, Nidderdale, Norfolk Coast, North Devon, North Pennines, North Wessex Downs, Northumberland Coast, Quantock Hills, Shropshire Hills, Solway Coast, South Devon, Suffolk Coast and Heaths, Surrey Hills, Tamar Valley.

3 Wye Valley.

4 Antrim Coast and Glens, Binevenagh, Causeway Coast, Lagan Valley, Mourne, Ring of Gullion, Sperrin, Strangford Lough.

5 https://www.gov.uk/guidance/areas-of-outstanding-natural-beauty-aonbs-designation-and-management

- Scenic quality, such as striking coastal landforms
- Relative wildness, such as distance from housing or having few roads
- Relative tranquillity, where natural sounds such as streams or birdsong are predominant
- Natural heritage features, such as distinctive geology or species and habitat
- Cultural heritage, which can include the built environment that makes the area unique, such as archaeological remains or historic parkland

1.9 Section 83 of the 2000 Act, 'Procedure for designation orders', provides that where Natural England or the NRBW proposes to make a designation order under section 82, they must consult every local authority whose area includes any part of the area to which the proposed area is to relate.

1.10 Before making the order, Natural England or the NRBW must publish notice of the proposals in the London Gazette and in one or more of the local newspapers in the area of each affected authority, stating the time within and manner in which representations may be made about the proposed order. Any representations duly made must be considered. The order, including any unresolved representations or objections, must then be submitted to the Secretary of State or the National Assembly for Wales, as the case may be, for confirmation. The Secretary of State or the Assembly can confirm the order either as submitted or with modifications, or can refuse to confirm the order. Where the order is refused or where it is determined that it be confirmed but with modifications, the Secretary of State/Assembly must consult National England/the NRBW and every local authority whose area includes any land to which the order relates, either as it was submitted or as it is proposed to be modified.

1.11 A designation order can be subsequently revoked or varied by a subsequent order under s82. The Secretary of State or Assembly can also, without prejudice to Natural England or the NRBW's powers under s82, make an order to vary any order made by Natural England or the NRBW. Occasionally, the government may decide to expand the area of an AONB. For example, on 7 July 2020 the Suffolk Coast and Heaths AONB was extended by c. 38km$^2$, to include areas such as the Stour Estuary.[6]

## 2 MANAGEMENT AND CONSERVATION BOARDS

2.1 Section 84 of the 2000 Act applies certain provisions of the National Parks and Access to the Countryside Act 1949 ("the 1949 Act") to AONBs in the same way as they apply to National Parks. These include: the duty of Natural England or the NRBW to give advice in connection with development matters (s6(4)(e) of the 1949 Act), consultation in connection with a development plan (s9 of the 1949 Act), and consultation in connection with access orders (s65(5) and (5A) of the 1949 Act).

2.2 Further, s84(4) provides that a local planning authority whose area consists of or includes the whole or any part of an AONB has the power, in keeping with the purpose of designating land as an AONB, to take "…all such action as appears to them expedient for the accomplishment of the purpose of conserving and enhancing the natural beauty of the area of outstanding natural beauty or so much of it as is included in their area".

2.3 This reflects the fact that, unlike with National Parks, the primary responsibility for the protection and promotion of AONBs lies with the local authorities within whose area they have been established, although s85 provides that any public body, as well as any minister of the Crown, person holding public

6 See the government announcement at: https://www.gov.uk/government/news/boost-for-picturesque-landscapes-as-suffolk-coast-and-heaths-area-of-outstanding-natural-beauty-extended

office, or statutory undertaker, shall in exercising any functions in relation to or so as to affect land in an AONB, have regard to the purpose of conserving and enhancing the natural beauty of the AONB.

2.4 The strategic issues that arise, and the duty to prepare management plans (see further below), are commonly addressed through the creation of AONB partnerships by which the relevant local authorities agree to pool resources and expertise. The officers and staff specifically allocated to these tasks are sometimes known as 'AONB units'. An AONB partnership could be a joint advisory committee or an AONB committee.

2.5 Each AONB must have a plan, known as an "area of outstanding natural beauty management plan" pursuant to s89(4) of the 2000 Act, which must be in place within three years of the designation, and a review must take place within five years of the start of the plan (see ss89(2) and (9) of the 2000 Act), although this will not apply where, before the end of the three or five-year period, as the case may be, a conservation board is established for the AONB (see further below). The plan must formulate the local authority's policy for the management of the AONB and for the carrying out of its functions in relation to it. Where an AONB covers more than one local authority, the plan is produced by all relevant authorities, acting jointly.

2.6 In Northern Ireland, the NIEA facilitates the management of AONBs by putting in place management plans and mechanisms.

2.7 The purpose of the management plan is to consider the conservation and enhancement of the natural beauty of the AONB with continuity and consistency over time. It will need to include[7]:

7 https://www.gov.uk/guidance/areas-of-outstanding-natural-beauty-aonbs-designation-and-management#development

- an *assessment* of the special quality of the AONB, such as a landscape character assessment that includes its condition and vulnerability to change
- *cross reference* to existing plans, such as local transport plans or biodiversity action plans
- a *strategy*, such as a 5-year plan, of how change will be managed
- *other special sites* that exist in the AONB, such as scheduled ancient monuments or sites of special scientific interest
- an *action plan*, for who will be doing what, why and by when
- a *monitoring plan* to show how the AONB's condition and effectiveness of management will be measured

2.8 Where it is thought that the size and complexity of an AONB will make informal mechanisms impracticable, a conservation board may be established under section 86 of the 2000 Act.

2.9 It is the Secretary of State (for England) or the National Assembly (for Wales) which may establish a conservation board to carry out the functions conferred by or under Part IV of the 2000 Act. A conservation board is established by order (s88).

2.10 Before such an order is made in England, the Secretary of State shall consult Natural England and every local authority whose area consists of or includes the whole or part of the AONB, and must not make the order unless satisfied that the majority of those local authorities consent (s86(6) of the 2000 Act). Section 86(7) makes equivalent provision in respect of the National Assembly and the requirement to consult the NRBW. Similarly, an order amending revoking a previous order made under s86(1) to establish a conservation board, may be made only after consultation with the conservation board to which it relates in addition to the consultation required by ss86(6) and (7).

2.11 Schedule 13 to the 2000 Act provides for the constitution of conservation boards. It is a body corporate, and consists of the number of local authority members, and members appointed by either the Secretary of State or National Assembly, as may be specified in the order, and also (in the case of an English board) parish members (appointed either by the parish council or parish meeting). However, the local authority members must be at least 40% of the total membership, and in the case of an English board, at least 20% of the total members must be parish members (Sch 13, para 3). The local authority and parish members must be of those authorities and parishes wholly or partly comprised in the AONB. A local authority must have regard to the desirability of appointing members who represent wards (in England) or electoral divisions (in Wales) situated wholly or partly in the relevant AONB.

2.12 Natural England/the NRBW must be consulted before any member is appointed to the conservation board. Terms of office are from one to three years and those ceasing to hold office are eligible for re-appointment (Sch 13, para 6).

2.13 In the exercise of its functions, it is the duty of the conservation board, by virtue of s87(1) of the 2000 Act, to have regard to (a) the purpose of conserving and enhancing the natural beauty of the AONB, and (b) the purpose of increasing the understanding and enjoyment by the public of the special qualities of the AONB. However, purpose '(b)' must give way to purpose '(a)' in that the board must attach greater weight to '(a)'if it appear to it that there is a conflict between the two purposes: see Chapter 1 for a fuller discussion of what is called the Sandford Principle.

2.14 Whilst having regard to the s87(1) purposes, a conservation board "shall seek to foster the economic and social well-being of local communities within the area of outstanding natural beauty and shall for that purpose co-operate with local authorities and public bodies whose functions include the promotion of economic or social development within the area of outstanding natural beauty" (s87(2)). The board's powers include the power to do anything which in its opinion is calculated to facilitate, or is conducive or incidental to, the accomplishment of the s87(1) purposes or the carrying out of any functions conferred on it by any other provision of Part IV of the 2000 Act or any other enactment.

2.15 Section 86(3) of the 2000 Act provides that where the Secretary of State or the National Assembly considers its expedient for either of the s87(1) purposes, then an order under s86(1) may provide for the transfer to the conservation board to which the s86 order relates, of any of the functions of local authorities so far as they relate to the AONB in question. Alternatively, it may be provided that any function of a local authority relating to the AONB in question is to be exercisable concurrently by the local authority and the conservation board.

2.16 However, the power in s86(3) does not apply to the functions of a local authority under Parts III (control of development), VII (enforcement) or XIII (application of the Act to Crown land) of the Town and Country Planning Act 1990 or to Parts 2 (local development) or 6 (Wales) of the Planning and Compulsory Purchase Act 2004.

2.17 Schedule 14 to the 2000 Act (entitled 'Supplemental powers of conservation boards') provides that a conservation board may acquire land, whether inside or outside its AONB and, subject to certain restrictions set out in paras (4) and (5) in the case of commons, open spaces and short tenancies, dispose of land held which is no longer required for the purposes of its function.

2.18 There are only two established Conservation Boards: see the Chilterns Area of Outstanding Natural Beauty (Establishment of Conservation Board) Order 2004/1778[8] and the Cotswolds Area

8 Amended by SI 2009/1578.

of Outstanding Natural Beauty (Establishment of Conservation Board) Order 2004/1777[9].

2.19 Conservation boards must also prepare, publish and keep under review management plans, as provided for by ss89 and 90 of the 2000 Act. Section 89(1) provides that a plan which formulates the board's policy for the management of its AONB and the carrying out of its functions in relation thereto must be prepared and published within two years of the date that the board was established. Alternatively, the board could within six months of the date of its establishment adopt as its AONB management plan one already prepared by the relevant local authority and publish that (s89(6)). Section 89(7) provides that the board must review its AONB management plan before the end of the period of five years since the plan was published, and thereafter at intervals of not more than five years. However, where the board has adopted its plan under s89(6), the first review must take place within three years of the date that the plan was published.

2.20 When a review of an AONB management plan takes place (whether by the local authority/authorities or by the conservation board), it must be determined whether it would be expedient to make any amendments, and a report must be published on the review, specifying any amendments that were considered appropriate: s89(10).

2.21 Section 90(2) requires that a copy of every plan, notice or report which is required to be published under s89 shall be sent to the Secretary of State/National Assembly.

2.22 Section 90 also provides that where the conservation board or relevant local authority proposes to publish, adopt or review any management plan under s89, it must give notice of the proposal to Natural England or the NRBW, as appropriate, and in the case of a conservation board, to every local authority whose area is wholly or partly comprised in the AONB. A copy of the plan

9 Amended by SI 2009/1579.

must be sent along with any proposed amendments, and any observations made by those bodies notified must be taken into consideration.

2.23 A further requirement in relation to AONBs in Wales (s90(1A)) is that the conservation board or relevant local authority proposing to publish, adopt or review any plan under s89 must have regard to the state of natural resources report as published under s8 of the Environment (Wales) Act 2016, and any area statement published under s11 of that Act for an area that includes all or part of the AONB.

2.24 AONB management plans can be used to help shape local plans including neighbourhood plans.

## 3 ROLE IN PLANNING

3.1 Section 85 of the 2000 Act provides that any public body exercising any functions in relation to or affecting land in an AONB shall have regard to the purpose of conserving and enhancing the natural beauty of the AONB.

3.2 Only the Secretary of State or the local planning authority can give permission for development in or affecting an AONB; as noted above, the local authority's development control functions under Part III TCPA 1990 may not pass to a conservation board.

3.3 In Northern Ireland, the Development Management Team provides advice on large-scale development proposals that may have a significant impact on the landscape character of an AONB. Planning policies for development proposals within AONBs are set out in the Planning Strategy for Rural Northern Ireland 1993.

3.4 In the NPPF (2019), which is a material consideration in the determination of planning applications, AONBs are provided for in paragraph 172 (covered in Chapter 4 of this book), which states that "great weight" should be given to the conservation and enhancement of the landscape and scenic beauty of AONBs, as well as National Parks and the Broads, which "have the highest status of protection in relation to these issues". The scale and extent of development within these areas should be "limited" and planning permission should be refused for "major development" other than in exceptional circumstances and where it can be demonstrated that the development is in the public interest. Whether a proposal is major development is a matter for the decision maker taking into account its nature, scale and setting, and whether it could have a significant adverse impact on the purposes for which the area has been designated or defined (see footnote 55 NPPF (2019)).

3.5 According to paragraph 172, consideration of applications for development should include an assessment of: a) the need for the development, including in terms of any national considerations, and the impact of permitting it, or refusing it, upon the local economy; b) the cost of, and scope for, developing outside the designated area, or meeting the need for it in some other way; and c) any detrimental effect on the environment, the landscape and recreational opportunities, and the extent to which that could be moderated.

3.6 Whilst the NPPF (2019) reflects the general presumption in favour of sustainable development (see paragraph 11), this is subject to policies in the Framework which protect areas or assets of particular importance where they provide a "clear reason" for refusing the development proposed. Those policies include those relating to AONBs (see footnote 6).

3.7 Planning Policy Wales (Edition 10, December 2018) discusses AONBs at paras. 6.3.5 to 6.3.10 under the heading 'landscape', again noting that "great weight" (6.3.7) should be given to conserving and enhancing AONBs, and their special qualities. Both NPs and AONBs must be afforded "the highest status of protection from inappropriate developments" (6.3.8). Again, major developments, should not take place except in exceptional circumstances which may arise after "rigorous examination" to demonstrate an overriding public need, that refusal would be "severely detrimental" to the local economy and that there is "no potential" for locating the development elsewhere or meeting the need in some other way (6.3.10). The policy protection in this document is therefore worded in more stringent terms than in the NPPF.[10]

3.8 The Strategic Planning Policy Statement for Northern Ireland (2015) ("SPPS") states at paragraph 6.187 that development proposals in AONBs must be sensitive to the distinctive special character of the area and the quality of the landscape, heritage and wildlife. Paragraph 6.188 provides that in assessing proposals, including cumulative impacts in such areas, account will also be taken of the Landscape Character Assessments and any other relevant guidance including AONB management plans. *Planning Policy Statement 2: Natural Heritage* (2013) preceded the SPPS but is still in use. Policy NH6 "Areas of Outstanding Natural Beauty" states that planning permission for new development within an AONB will only be granted where it is of appropriate design, size and scale for the locality and all of the specified criteria are met. These include the requirement that the siting and scale of the proposal is sympathetic to the character of the AONB in general and of the particular locality. The explanatory text at paragraphs 5.14 and 5.16 is identical to that in paragraphs 6.187 and 6.188 of the SPPS.[11]

10 See Chapter 4 for more detail.

11 See Chapter 4.

# CHAPTER FOUR

# THE APPLICATION OF NATIONAL POLICY AND GUIDANCE

*James Maurici QC and Jacqueline Lean*

## 1. INTRODUCTION

1.1 In this chapter we consider the policy position in England, Wales and Northern Ireland. Sections 1 – 6 discuss English policy and the relevant provisions of NPPF (2019) and relevant guidance. Welsh policy (discussed in Section 7 and 8) in particular has a number of similarities to (but also some differences from) the English policy. This means that some of the case-law and appeal decisions discussed below on the NPPF will also be at least relevant in Wales, and may also be relevant in Northern Ireland. Northern Ireland is considered at Sections 9 and 10).

## 2 THE NATIONAL PLANNING POLICY FRAMEWORK

2.1 The NPPF (2019) makes the following provision for NPs, the Broads and AONBs:

(a) Para. 170 of the NPPF recognises "the intrinsic character and beauty of the countryside";

(b) Para. 11 of the NPPF, dealing with the presumption in favour of sustainable development, excludes the presumption where "the application of policies in this Framework that protect areas or assets of particular importance provides a clear reason for refusing the development proposed" – these are then exclusively defined in footnote 6 and include "an Area of Outstanding Natural Beauty, a National Park (or within the Broads Authority)";

(c) Para. 63 provides "[p]rovision of affordable housing should not be sought for residential developments that are not major developments, other than in designated rural areas (where policies may set out a lower threshold of 5 units or fewer ...". "Designated rural areas" is defined in the glossary of the NPPF (2019) as "National Parks, Areas of Outstanding Natural Beauty and areas designated as 'rural' under Section 157 of the Housing Act 1985".

(d) Para. 71 provides "Local planning authorities should support the development of entry-level exception sites, suitable for first time buyers (or those looking to rent their first home), unless the need for such homes is already being met within the authority's area. These sites should be on land which is not already allocated for housing and should: … b) be adjacent to existing settlements, proportionate in size to them, not compromise the protection given to areas or assets of particular importance in this Framework". These areas are defined in footnote 34 "i.e. the areas referred to in footnote 6. Entry-level exception sites should not be permitted in National Parks (or within the Broads Authority), Areas of Outstanding Natural Beauty or land designated as Green Belt."

(e) Para. 172 of the NPPF (2019) provides[1]:

> *"Great weight should be given to conserving and enhancing landscape and scenic beauty in National Parks, the Broads[2] and Areas of Outstanding Natural Beauty, which have the highest status of protection in relation to these issues. The conservation and enhancement of wildlife and cultural heritage are also important considerations in these areas, and should be given great weight in National Parks and the Broads. The scale and extent of development within these designated areas should be*

---

1 This replaced paras. 115 and 116 of the NPPF (2012) and was first included in the NPPF (2018), July 2018. The NPPF (2019) is identical in this regard to the NPPF (2018).

2 Footnote 54 of the NPPF (2019) provides "English National Parks and the Broads: UK Government Vision and Circular 2010 provides further guidance and information about their statutory purposes, management and other matters"

> *limited*[3]*. Planning permission should be refused for major development other than in exceptional circumstances, and where it can be demonstrated that the development is in the public interest. Consideration of such applications should include an assessment of:*
> *a) the need for the development, including in terms of any national considerations, and the impact of permitting it, or refusing it, upon the local economy;*
> *b) the cost of, and scope for, developing outside the designated area, or meeting the need for it in some other way; and*
> *c) any detrimental effect on the environment, the landscape and recreational opportunities, and the extent to which that could be moderated."*

"Major development" is now defined by footnote 55[4] as "For the purposes of paragraphs 172 and 173, whether a proposal is 'major development' is a matter for the decision maker, taking into account its nature, scale and setting, and whether it could have a significant adverse impact on the purposes for which the area has been designated or defined." [5]

(f) Para. 205 under the heading "Facilitating the sustainable use of minerals" says "When determining planning applications, great weight should be given to the benefits of mineral extraction, including to the economy. In considering proposals for mineral extraction, minerals planning authorities should: a) as far as is practical, provide for the maintenance of landbanks of non-energy minerals from outside National

[3] This sentence is new to the NPPF (2018) and (2019) see below.

[4] This definition also applies for the purposes of para. 173, in relation to "Heritage Coast".

[5] The footnote was introduced in the NPPF (2018), July 2018. The 2019 version made no changes to the paras. that are relevant for present purposes.

Parks, the Broads, Areas of Outstanding Natural Beauty and World Heritage Sites, scheduled monuments and conservation areas".

## 3 MAJOR DEVELOPMENT

### Introduction

3.1 In determining whether to or not to grant planning permission in a NP, the Boards or an AONB the first matter that must be determined is whether what is proposed is "major development" as defined in para. 172. If it is then planning permission should be refused for major development other than in exceptional circumstances, and where it can be demonstrated that the development is in the public interest. However, even when development is not defined as "major development" for these purposes that does not mean that permission will in any way necessarily be granted. Para. 172 advises that in relation to any development (major or not) "[g]reat weight should be given to conserving and enhancing landscape and scenic beauty in National Parks, the Broads and Areas of Outstanding Natural Beauty, which have the highest status of protection in relation to these issues". Moreover, it advises that "the conservation and enhancement of wildlife and cultural heritage are also important considerations in these areas, and should be given great weight in National Parks and the Broads". Para. 172 also makes clear that as an overall objective the "scale and extent of development within these designated areas should be limited"[6], and it is for this reason that major development is subject to an even stricter set of policy tests.

## Some materials that are of assistance in considering the meaning of "major development"

3.2 The following documents are key in considering the meaning of "major development":

---

[6] In R (Advearse) v Dorset Council v Hallam Land Management Ltd. [2020] EWHC 807 (Admin) it was argued that that the new words place a further restriction on major development in the designated areas; that the scale and extent of any such development must also be limited. Swift J rejected this holding:

> *"34. ... Advearse relies on the consultation document published by the Secretary of State in March 2018 that first set out the new words in what was at that stage, paragraph 170 in Part 15 of a new draft NPPF. The material part of the narrative in that consultation document said this*
> *"This chapter has been updated to align with the 25-year Environmental Plan. It includes additional policy on strengthening existing networks of habitats (paragraph 169) and taking air quality fully into account (paragraph 180), clarifies that development within National Parks and Areas of Outstanding Natural Beauty should be limited (paragraph 170); and also clarifies the implications for policy on areas defined as Heritage Coast (paragraph 171)".*
> *35. I do not accept Advearse's submission that the new words amount to any material change of policy relevant to the Council's decision on the application for planning permission for the Vearse Farm Development. Paragraph 172 of NPPF 2019, like its predecessor paragraph 116 of NPPF 2012 treats major development as a discrete class of development. In NPPF 2019, Footnote 55 to paragraph 172 states that it is for the decision-maker to decide whether or not an application before it is an application for major development "taking account of its nature, scale and setting, and whether it could have a significant adverse impact on the purposes for which the area had been designated or defined." That explanation was not on the face of NPPF 2012 but it is no more than a natural explanation of the application of what was then paragraph 116 of NPPF 2012. Since "major development" was not a defined term what amounted to major development could only have been a matter of assessment for the decision-maker. Even without the new words it was clear from NPPF 2012 that major development would be "exceptional". Further, it was clear from sub-paragraphs (a) - (c), which set out mandatory considerations, that no permission should be given for major development save to the extent the development was needed in the public interest, met a need that*

(a) The NPPF (2019) itself: para. 172 and footnote 55;

(b) The PPG in relation to "major development".[7] This states: *"All development in National Parks, the Broads and Areas of Outstanding Beauty will need to be located and designed in a way that reflects their status as landscapes of the highest quality. Where applications for major development come forward, paragraph 172 of the Framework sets out a number of particular*

---

*could not be addressed elsewhere or in some other way, and met that need in a way that to the extent possible, moderated detrimental effect on the environment, the landscape, and recreational opportunities. Those mandatory considerations, of themselves, embodied (and in paragraph 172 of NPPF 2019 continue to embody) a principle of limited development.*

*36. Reading paragraph 172 of NPPF 2019 as a whole, it is clear that the new words are not directed to the class of major development. Rather, those words are directed to development outside that class, and apply to such development the same principle of limited development that already applied to major development. Hence the description in the consultation document of the new words as "clarifying" what was already implicit in paragraph 115 and 116 of NPPF 2012.*

*37. In its submissions Advearse referred me to the judgment of Holgate J in Monkhill Ltd v Secretary of State for Housing Communities and Local Government [2019] EWHC 1993 (Admin) and in particular paragraphs 8, 9 and 51 of that judgment. However, I can see nothing in that judgment which is at odds with anything I have said above. If the present paragraph 172 NPPF 2019 were notionally divided into two parts to reflect the previous division between paragraphs 115 and 116 NPPF 2012, the function performed by the new words is only to make clear that a principle of limited development applies to developments regardless of whether the development is or is not classed as major development.*

*38. The consequence in this case is that Advearse's second ground of challenge fails. I do not consider that the words added into paragraph 172 NPPF 2019 when compared to the previous paragraphs 115 and 116 of NPPF 2012 identified any material change of policy within the NPPF that affected the Vearse Farm Development. At the Committee meeting on 2 November 2017 the Officer's Report approached the decision on the premise that the proposed development of Vearse Farm amounted to major development for the purposes of what was then paragraph 116 of NPPF 2012. I accept that this was also the basis on which the Planning Committee reached its decision at its meeting. Therefore, there was no need as at 2 May 2019 when the planning permission was granted, for the Council to revisit the decision the Planning Committee had taken on 2 November 2017 because of any change in the NPPF."*

*considerations that should apply when deciding whether permission should be granted*"[8];

(c) The National Parks Circular, "English National Parks and the Broads: UK government vision and circular 2010" ("the NP Circular") (see below) which says in relation to "major development" that:

> *"31. Major development in or adjacent to the boundary of a Park can have a significant impact on the qualities for which they were designated. Government planning policy towards the Parks is that major development should not take place within a Park except in exceptional circumstances. This is set out in Planning Policy Statement 7: Sustainable Development in Rural Areas and restated in Minerals Policy Statement 1: Planning and Minerals. Applications for all major developments should be subject to the most rigorous examination and proposals should be demonstrated to be in the public interest before being allowed to proceed. The criteria for the*

---

[7] See further below.

[8] See Para.: 041 Reference ID: 8-041-20190721, Revision date: 21 07 2019. The PPG previously offered more guidance on these matters but this has been removed:

> *"How is major development defined in National Parks and Areas of Outstanding Natural Beauty, for the purposes of the consideration of planning applications in these areas?*
> *Planning permission should be refused for major development in a National Park, the Broads or an Area of Outstanding Natural Beauty except in exceptional circumstances and where it can be demonstrated to be in the public interest. Whether a proposed development in these designated areas should be treated as a major development, to which the policy in paragraph 172 of the Framework applies, will be a matter for the relevant decision taker, taking into account the proposal in question and the local context. The Framework is clear that great weight should be given to conserving landscape and scenic beauty in these designated areas irrespective of whether the policy in paragraph 172 is applicable."* (see Para.: 005 Reference ID: 8-005-20140306; Revision date: 06 03 2014).

> *assessment of such applications is currently set out in Paragraph 14 of Minerals Policy Statement 1 and Paragraph 22 of Planning Policy Statement 7*[9]*. The Government expects all public authorities with responsibility for the regulation of development in the Parks to apply the test rigorously, liaising together to ensure that it is well understood by developers."*

(d) The so-called "Maurici Opinions" as they have become known on the meaning of "major development" in a NP, written for the South Downs National Park Authority which published them on the Internet. These have been much publicised, argued about on planning appeals/applications and considered by High Court in R(Green) v SDNPA [2018] EWHC 604 (Admin):

i first opinion – on PPS7 in 2011: https://www.southdowns.gov.uk/wp-content/uploads/2015/01/Legal-Opinion-of-Major-Development-June-2011.pdf;

ii second opinion – on NPPF (2012) in 2014: https://www.southdowns.gov.uk/wp-content/uploads/2015/01/Guidelines-on-Significance-for-SDNP-Planning-Applications-–-NPPF-Complaint-July-2014.pdf;

(e) The following cases:

i Aston v SSCLG [2014] 2 P&CR 10;

ii R (Forge Field Society) v Sevenoaks DC [2015] JPL 22.

iii R (Cherkley Campaign) v Mole Valley DC [2014] EWCA Civ 567;

---

9 See now the NPPF (2019) and see below on PPS7.

iv Green – see above;

v R (Steer) v Shepway DC [2018] EWHC 238 (Admin)[10];

(f) The report by Sheffield Hallam University for the Campaign for National Parks entitled "An examination of the development and implementation of planning policy relating to major development in the English and Welsh National Parks" dated November 2016: https://www.cnp.org.uk/blog/investigating-major-development-test (hereinafter "the Major Development Report").

(g) The Major Development Report also found that some National Parks in England and Wales had local interpretations of "major development" in their local plans, and some did not.

## "Major development": a potted history

3.3 There has been Government guidance on "major development" in NPs since the 1949 Act. The so-called Silkin test was laid

---

[10] In Steer planning permission was granted for the development of a holiday park in AONB. The development would include the construction of 12 holiday lodges, a reception building, a store building, formation of a fishing lake, a car park, tennis courts, a children's play area and a putting green. The Officer Report ("OR") said it could be "major development" but that "an Inspector could formulate a different view on this at appeal." At no point did the OR the Committee conclusively determine whether or not the proposals were "major development". Lang J. held that "the question as to whether or not this particular proposal was a "major development" could have been decided either way, on the evidence. On the one hand, there would only be twelve lodges, but on the other hand, this was a sizeable holiday park, with construction of a reception building, a store, a fishing lake, a car park, tennis courts, a children's play area and a putting green, on what was agricultural land, located next to a wood classified as Ancient Woodland". The Judge found that there was "real doubt" as to whether the members in fact gave proper consideration to whether para. 116 of NPPF (2012) applied. Ultimately, "because of the lack of any reliable record of the meeting" she was not satisfied, on the balance of probabilities, that they did not do so. Therefore "since the burden of proof rests on the Claimant" the challenge on this ground failed.

down in 1949 – see the Major Development Report at section 1.2:

> *"... national planning policy on major development in national parks (and Areas of Outstanding Natural Beauty) focusses on what is commonly known as the 'major development test' (MDT). The MDT sets out a framework for deciding whether or not a major development application should be permitted. The original MDT was laid down by Lewis Silkin, Minister for Town and Country Planning, in 1949, and was designed to protect the amenity of national parks from minerals development. The so-called Silkin test had a presumption against development except where:*
>
> *i. exploitation was "absolutely" necessary in the national interest;*
>
> *ii. it must be clear beyond all doubt that there was no possible alternative source of supply;*
>
> *iii. and, if those two conditions are satisfied, the permission must be subject to the condition that restoration of the site would be undertaken at the earliest possible opportunity.*
>
> *(MacEwen and MacEwen 1982 p233)*
>
> *The post-war and subsequent governments verbally endorsed the Silkin test as a statement of government policy, but have also modified it over time"*

3.4 The major development test was then incorporated into PPG7 in the early 1990s. In the 2000s it was included in PPS7 – the subject of the first Maurici Opinion (see above).

3.5 There are two things to note on this history. First, there was never any definition of "major development" for these purposes in any policy from 1949 up to July 2018, when NPPF (2018) was published. Second, the language/test where something is "major development" has changed over time. Thus, PPS7 used to say "applications for all such development proposals should be subject to the most rigorous examination", that is not included in the NPPF[11], albeit surely this must remain the case. Moreover, PPG7 used to refer to "major development proposals, which are more national than local in character" (emphasis added). This wording suggested that major development was by definition of a national character, that was removed from PPS7 but is still part of Welsh national policy: see Chapter 4B.

3.6 The text on major developments in what is now para 172 of the NPPF (2019), see above, is very similar to what as was included in para. 116 of the NPPF (2012). What is new is one sentence (see above) and, more importantly, footnote 55 which provides the definition of "major development". This was absent from the NPPF (2012), which like PPS7 and other policy before it, said nothing about what was "major development".

## The Meaning of "Major Development"

3.7 There is, and has been for some time, a definition of "major development" in what is now the Town and Country Planning (Development Management Procedure) Order 2015 ("the DMPO")[12]:

> *""major development" means development involving any one or more of the following—*
> *(a) the winning and working of minerals or the use of land for mineral-working deposits;*
> *(b) waste development;*
> *(c) the provision of dwellinghouses where—*

---

[11] It remains in the Welsh national policy: see below. The test in Planning Policy Wales is basically the text from PPG7.

[12] Earlier versions of the DMPO, and before that the General Procedure Development Order as was, contained similar provision.

*(i) the number of dwellinghouses to be provided is 10 or more; or*
*(ii) the development is to be carried out on a site having an area of 0.5 hectares or more and it is not known whether the development falls within sub-paragraph (c)(i);*
*(d) the provision of a building or buildings where the floor space to be created by the development is 1,000 square metres or more; or*
*(e) development carried out on a site having an area of 1 hectare or more;"*

3.8 It became well-established in case-law that this definition did not apply directly to the meaning of major development in the context of national policy on NPs, the Broads and AONBs (then set out in para. 116 of the NPPF (2012)): see Aston[13] and Forge Field[14].

---

13 In this case planning permission was granted on appeal for 14 dwellings in an AONB. C argued that "major development" in para. 116 of the NPPF had meaning in the DMPO e.g. in this regard 10+ dwellings. The Inspector rejected this and said development of 14 dwellings could not properly be described as "major" "by any published or even common sense criterion". This was challenged in the High Court, Wyn Williams J. held: "... appropriate that the term should be construed in the context of the document in which it appears. In my judgment the context of the NPPF and paragraphs 115 and 116 in particular militate against the precise definition which [C] suggests should attach to the phrase "major development". The word major has a natural meaning in the English language albeit not one that is precise. In my judgment to define "major development" as precisely as suggested by [C] would mean that the phrase has an artificiality which would not be appropriate in the context of national planning policy". He said "I am satisfied that the Inspector made no error of law when he determined that the meaning of the phrase major development was that which would be understood from the normal usage of those words".

14 Planning permission was granted by the local planning authority for 6 dwellings in an AONB. The Officer Report ("OR") seemed to suggest that the officer had concluded it was not major development because it did not exceed 10 dwellings as per the DMPO definition. C challenged this on basis that this an error post-Aston. The claim failed; Lindblom J. held:

(i) the view of officer that this was not major development was "consistent with common sense";

3.9 The 'Maurici Opinions', see above, were provided to the South Downs National Park Authority in 2011 and 2014 in the context of PPS7 and NPPF (2012). Although, the NPPF has been amended since the Maurici Opinions were drafted[15] and these have been subjected to detailed consideration by the High Court in Green[16] nonetheless the essential points in the Maurici Opinions, in our view, still hold good. As the July 2014 Opinion stated:

> *"23. In light of the caselaw, guidance and appeal decisions since 2011, I consider that the views contained in my 2011 Opinion[17] remain, despite various developments in the caselaw and changes to policy, largely valid.*

---

(ii) it was wrong to import the DMPO meaning of "major development" into para. 116 of the NPPF (2012);
(iii) the "concept should be understood in the context of the document in which it appears, and in paragraphs 115 and 116 of the NPPF"
(iv) ""major developments" would normally be projects much larger than six dwellings on a site the size of Forge Field"
(v) whether something is a "major development" is an exercise of planning judgment.

15 Although there is no difference between the 2018 and 2019 versions relevant for present purposes.

16 In Green planning permission was granted for redevelopment of Grade II listed building into a hotel and restaurant (28 rooms) and associated facilities including staff accommodation and provision of parking spaces (68) within the South Downs NP. The decision was judicially reviewed it being alleged that the officer report ("OR") failed to correctly apply the test for major development in para. 116 of NPPF (2012). The OR referred to Maurici Opinions and noted "Mr Maurici's Opinions form part of a Member's training programme and the test of what amounts to a "major development" within the meaning of paragraph 116 is an issue which is often referred to in planning applications that come before the Defendant's Planning Committee" (see para. 15). The OR's conclusion on "major development" was said to be flawed for three reasons – all said to be contrary to the Maurici opinions:

(i) Failure to take into account the designation of the proposal as major development under the DMPO
(ii) Failure to consider "all the circumstances" as advised by, in particular the consultee responses identifying potential for serious adverse impacts.
(iii) Failure to fully consider the local context.
The Judge rejected the challenge.

17 An Opinion considering the meaning of "major development" in the context of PPS7.

*However, there are matters of nuance which need revision. Accordingly, I set out below a set of principles – derived from the caselaw, guidance and appeal decisions - to be applied by decision makers when determining whether an application is for "major development".*

*24. First, the overarching principle is that the determination of whether a proposal amounts to "major development" for the purposes of paragraph 116 of the NPPF is a matter of planning judgment to be decided by the decision maker in light of all the circumstances of the application and the context of the application site.*

*25. Secondly, the phrase "major development" is to be given its ordinary meaning. Accordingly, it would be wrong in law to:*
*a. Apply the definition of major development contained in the 2010 Order to paragraph 116 of the NPPF.*
*b. Apply any set or rigid criteria to defining "major development".*
*c. Restrict the definition to proposals that raise issues of national significance.*

*26. Thirdly, in making a determination as to whether the development is "major development", the decision maker may consider whether the development has the potential to have a serious adverse impact on the natural beauty and recreational opportunities provided by a National Park or AONB by reason of its scale, character or nature. However, that does not require (and ought not to include) an in-depth consideration of whether the development will in fact have such an impact. Instead, a prima facie assessment of the potential for such impact, in light of the scale, character or nature of the proposed development is sufficient.*

*27. Fourthly, as a matter of planning judgement, the decision maker must consider the application in its local context. This is made clear in the PPG, but also appears implicit in the caselaw. In* ***Forge Field****, for instance, Lindblom J noted that ""major developments" would normally be projects much larger than six dwellings on a site the size of Forge Field." In so observing, he appears to have contemplated the possibility that, depending on the local context, there may be circumstances in which a project of six dwellings could amount to major development on a site the size of Forge Field. Accordingly, in principle, the same development may amount to "major development" in one National Park, but not in another; or in one part of a National Park, but not in another part of the same National Park.*

*28. Fifthly, the application of criteria such as whether the development is EIA development, whether it falls within Schedule 2 of the Town and Country Planning (Environmental Impact Assessment) Regulations 1999 (as amended), whether it is "major development" for the purposes of the 2010 Order, or whether it requires the submission of an appraisal/assessment of the likely traffic, health, retail implications of the proposal will all be relevant considerations, but will not determine the matter and may not even raise a presumption either way.*

*29. Finally, and fundamentally, in making a determination, it is important to keep in mind the ordinary, common sense, meaning of the word "major". Although Lindblom J appears to have contemplated*

> *the theoretical possibility of 6 dwellings amounting to "major development" he noted (rightly in my opinion), that in ordinary language a "major development" will normally be much larger than housing units. Accordingly, having considered all the circumstances, including the local context, the decision maker must take a common sense view on whether the proposed development can appropriately be described – in ordinary language – as "major development".*

3.10 As noted above the Maurici Opinions were considered by Stuart-Smith J in the Green case. Stuart-Smith J largely approved the Maurici Opinions, save for two matters:

(a) Stuart-Smith J read the Maurici Opinions as saying that whether the development was defined as major in the DMPO was always relevant in deciding whether it was "major development" for the purposes of para. 116 of the NPPF (2012). He considered that this was incorrect, in that it might be relevant but was not always so. This constituted a misreading of the Maurici Opinions, which did not indicate that the definition in the DMPO would always be relevant, but only that, as the Judge held, they could be relevant. There are material considerations to which a decision-maker may choose to have regard, this is one of them;

(b) At para. 55, Stuart-Smith J stated "…I regard any distinction between "potential" for harm and "likelihood" of harm as sterile and unimportant. Any assessment of potential for harm necessarily includes some consideration of whether harm is likely; and if Mr Maurici meant[18] to advise that the existence of any possibility at all of serious harm would require any development to be categorised as a "major development" within the meaning of paragraph

[18] He did not!

[172], I would respectfully disagree". Again, this was not a correct reading of the Maurici Opinions; these do not advise that the existence of any possibility at all of serious harm would require any development to be categorised as a "major development".

3.11 The consultation draft of the proposed revised NPPF issued in 2018 indicated that the DMPO definition of major development would be applied in the context of the NPs, the Broads and AONBs. However, there were many objections to this proposal in the consultation process, in part by the NPAs themselves, which were concerned that if the threshold for major development is too low, then this would risk a consequential watering down of the exceptional circumstances/public interest test. The Government relented and changed its approach, albeit introducing footnote 55 into the revised NPPF.

3.12 There is, as yet, no clear or definitive guidance, either in policy or judicial authority, as to how the definition of 'major development' now contained in footnote 55 of the 2019 NPPF is to be construed. There are, moreover, no indicative thresholds as to the square footage or number of units which would 'usually' constitute major development (cf. the definitions in the 2015 Order), and any previous decisions as to whether a particular development would constitute 'major development' whilst informative cannot be regarded as 'precedent' (in the strict legal sense) as to whether a similar development elsewhere should also be regarded as major development.

## Applying the major development test

3.13 There has since the NPPF (2012) been many, many appeal decisions on the meaning of "major development" for the purposes of NPs, the Broads and AONBs. Most of these cases concern AONBs, with a small number concerned with NPs and the Broads. As we have said these are not in any way to be regarded as precedents[19]. They can only give a "feel" as to how the test is applied. Deciding what is major development is, as footnote 55, now makes clear a matter for the decision maker, taking into account its nature, scale and setting, and whether it could have a significant adverse impact on the purposes for which the area has been designated or defined.

3.14 Many of the post NPPF (2012) appeal decisions pre-date footnote 55. We also now have some Higher Courts case-law on the meaning of "major development", see above; although again this pre-dates footnote 55. Despite the "major development" test having been with us since 1949 there was no Higher Court case-law on its meaning until Aston in July 2013. There are now a number of cases. The reason for this recent explosion in Higher Court cases on the meaning of "major development" is a combination of the introduction of the NPPF (2012) (albeit that was in itself in no way radically different from PPS7 in this regard) and the Supreme Court's decision in Tesco Stores Ltd v Dundee [2012] P.T.S.R. 983 which held meaning of planning policy a question of law and thus generated, for first time, litigation on what was "major development" as defined in national policy.

3.15 Looking at the many appeal decisions since the NPPF (2012) in terms of housing schemes there is little that one can derive from this:

(a) Lindblom J (as he then was) in Forge Field suggested that "major developments" would normally be projects much larger than six dwellings, but this must depend on the particular circumstances;

---

19 See e.g. what was said by the Inspector in APP/K1128/W/18/3218474 and 19/3226585 at para. 26 and 27: "[e]ach case must be determined on its own merits. The appeal decisions from elsewhere are of little assistance as they relate to much larger settlements ...". See also APP/K1128/W/18/3215689 at para. 30 taking into account the local AONB Management Plan criteria in determining if the proposal for 15 homes was major development.

(b) Beyond that there are many, many appeals looking at housing schemes proposing 5 units and upwards with very different views being taken on whether the development was to be regarded as "major" or not. This is, of course, because whether something is "major development" depends on all the circumstances. Thus, there are appeal decisions finding that a proposal for 10 units was "major development" for these purposes (see APP/Q1153/W/16/3157958) and that a proposal for 38 units was not (see APP/G1630/W/15/31389514)[20].

3.16 In terms of non-housing appeals looking at this issue, relevant appeals include determinations that:

(a) The erection of new storage and warehousing buildings exceeding 1000 sq m of floorspace was regarded as major development;

(b) In APP/N2535/W/18/3200598, change of use to an open field to site 35 holiday lodge caravans and one site office/reception caravan in Lincolnshire Wolds AONB was found to constitute major development;

(c) In APP/X1118/W/15/3012049, an outline development was proposed in Ilfracombe for an Assisted Living residential scheme and associated works in an AONB. This was not found to constitute major development, but the appeal was rejected, the Inspector giving great weight should be given to conserving landscape and scenic beauty "irrespective of whether the development is considered to be major";

(d) APP/N2525/A/11/2164661: The Inspector decided 2 wind turbines were not "major development";

[20] See the attached annex for a list of examples. Thanks for this go to Alistair Mills of Landmark Chambers.

(e) APP/W0340/W/3157428: fly fishing training facility and an underground rifle range with associated facility building at the Royal Berkshire Shooting School was regarded as "major development";

(f) APP/D3830/W/16/3151730: 5MW solar array on a 15.1 ha site was regarded as major development;

(g) APP/X2600/A/13/2210509: A pet incinerator including the installation of a 200-litre fuel tank was found not to be major;

(h) APP/X2220/W/18/3194604: planning permission was sought in an AONB for erection of a water bottling plant including storage and offices (totalling around 1,800sqm of floorspace), new vehicular access, parking and turning areas, landscaping and biodiversity enhancements. The Inspector refused the appeal on the basis that the proposal would have "an unacceptable effect in relation to the AONB... regardless of whether the proposal is considered to be "major" or not"".

> *"21. … In this individual case, I consider that the proposal has an unacceptable effect in relation to the AONB and its effects on neighbours and this is regardless of whether the proposal is considered to be "major" or not. However, and for the purposes of clarity, taking account of the scale, character and nature of the proposal and the surrounding in which it would be constructed, as well as the effects that I have determined that it would have, I consider that it represents "major development" for the purposes of paragraph 172 of the NPPF."*

(i) APP/A1530/A/13/2195924: planning permission sought for 'The Stour Valley Visitor Centre at Horkesley Park' comprising a country park, art and craft studios (The Chantry), public gardens, a central building complex to provide an indoor display ring, 'Suffolk Punch Breeding Centre', entrance building, shop, café, 'Field to Fork', 'Farming through the ages', Active Learning, 'Nature Watch', and retained greenhouse as a demonstration nursery and gardens, an 'Energy Centre', main and overflow car parks, service yard, highway improvements, ancillary works and infrastructure provision". The Inspector held:

> *"the proposed development would include the erection of 8,950 m² of new buildings and the change of use of some 42 ha of agricultural land to country park. It is intended to attract more than 300,000 visitors every year from across the region and more specifically from China. It would by any measure be a major development ... However, the new buildings would occupy the site of the redundant nursery, outside the AONB ... They would form the major part of the new development. While there would be the creation of the Chinese garden, the erection of fencing and the change of use of land within the AONB, these are relatively minor elements of the scheme in terms of development. The proposal cannot with any factual accuracy be described as major development in the AONB, so in my view ¶116 of the Framework cannot be invoked".*

The Secretary of State agreed that it was not major development in the AONB (see the Secretary of State's decision letter at para. 17).

(j) In <u>Cherkley</u> Richards LJ said "I do not think that the creation of one fairway and one tee of a golf course could reasonably be regarded as a major development in the AONB, even when account is taken of the fact that they form part of a larger golf course development the rest of which is immediately adjacent to the AONB".

3.17 Footnote 55 in defining "major development" says that it is "a matter for the decision maker, taking into account its nature, scale and setting, and whether it could have a significant adverse impact on the purposes for which the area has been designated or defined", as was noted in the Maurici Opinions this means that the very same development might be regarded as "major development" in one protected area and not another. Of course, the fact that there is any definition is a departure from the position that has prevailed since 1949. On one view though this definition is not seeking to be radical: (i) it confirms that what is "major development" is a matter of judgment for decision-maker; (ii) it requires that regard must be had to the "nature, scale and setting"; and (iii) it indicates that consideration also needs to be given to "whether it could have a significant adverse impact on the purposes for which the area has been designated or defined". This is clearly consistent with the previous approach as set out in the Maurici opinions and the case-law discussed above.

3.18 It is clear that as before the definition of "major development" in the DMPO is not the definition for the purposes of para, 172 of the NPPF. However, the glossary to the NPPF (2019) retained the definition of "Major development" as being "For housing, development where 10 or more homes will be provided, or the site has an area of 0.5 hectares or more. For non-residential development it means additional floorspace of 1,000m2 or more, or a site of 1 hectare or more, or as otherwise provided in the Town and Country Planning (Development Management Procedure) (England) Order 2015". Moreover, "Major development" is referred to in other paras. of NPPF (2019) not in context of NPs, the Broads and AONBs: so see paras. 63, 64, 76 (all housing) and 165 (flooding). There is a residual concern as to whether this general definition for other purposes in the NPPF may influence meaning of "major development" under para 172.

3.19 There are some post-footnote 55 appeal decisions that are a concern in this regard e.g.:

(a) APP/K1128/W/18/3208541, Land to the east of Lyte Lane West Charleton, Kingsbridge (26 March 2019): planning permission was sought for 24 dwellings (including affordable housing), village green, children's play area, parking area and associated works including landscaping. The site was in an AONB. The Inspector held that it was "major development" because: (i) it would be major development under DMPO which the Inspector equated with being the position relating to development outside an AONB; and (ii) "Mindful of the great weight otherwise to be given to conservation and enhancement of AONBs I see no basis as to why this footnote should be considered to promote a definition of major development that was, as a matter of course, larger outside the AONB";

(b) APP/D0840/W/18/3208554 and APP/D0840/W/18/3213658, Land South of Tregellast Parc, St Keverne (7 March 2019): planning permission was sought in an AONB for (1) a sustainable residential development of 10 dwellings and associated vehicular access; and (2) affordable housing led development of up to 10 dwellings, site access and associated landscaping. The Inspector dismissed the appeal having concluded that the proposal constituted major development in the AONB. It was said "Paragraph 172 of the revised Framework also advises that planning permission should be refused for major development other than in exceptional circumstances. Housing schemes of 10 or more dwellings are generally classified within the Glossary of the revised Framework as major development, and with regard to footnote 55 I see no reason why the proposed schemes should be considered otherwise in this case."

In our view both these decisions are plainly wrong. It seems the definition elsewhere in NPPF (2019) of "major development" is unduly influencing the para. 172 definition. So, the effect of these two appeal decisions is that the DMPO definition was basically applied under para. 172. This is contrary to what is intended.

3.20 For the correct approach see:

(a) APP/J3530/W/17/3172629, Brickfield Barns, Saxmundham Road, Alceburgh Suffolk (21 November 2018). In that case planning permission was sought in an AONB for demolition of existing redundant stores, change of use of builder's yard and the redevelopment of quarry site to provide 43 dwellings (including 14 affordable). The Inspector noted that the NPPF (2018) is clear that there is a separate definition for "major development" within an AONB (emphases added):

> "56. *At the time of the application Council officers concluded that the proposal was major development, but considered that the public benefits arising form the provision of the proposed dwellings in this location, were sufficiently 'exceptional' to justify the proposal. In reaching a judgement on this matter they had regard to the definition within The Town and Country Planning (Development Management Procedure) (England) Order 2010. This definition includes developments of 10 dwellings or more. <u>The 2018 Framework is clear that this definition is not the basis for assessing whether a scheme is major development within an AONB.</u>*[21]"

The Inspector nonetheless found what was proposed to be "major development": "The appeal scheme would be a substantial extension to a small market town and would considerably exceed the 10 dwellings allocated in the [Development Plan]. The amount of new buildings and the extent of the access road, footways, hard surfaced areas and

[21] The 2019 NPPF is the same for these purposes.

other infrastructure would be of a significant scale in this part of the AONB". This approach: (i) in recognising that "major development" in para. 172 has a different definition to "major development" for other purposes is, in our view, correct; and the decision as to why what was proposed was "major" is entirely orthodox: it looked at all the potential impacts.

(b) APP/K1128/W/17/3185418, Proposed phase 2 development site, Mill Lane, Frogmore, Kingsbridge, Devon, TQ7 2PA (decision date 17 August 2018): planning permission was sought for 28 dwellings (including affordable/starter homes), community allotments, accesses, highway improvements and associated landscaping. The site formed part of the open countryside surrounding Frogmore and was situated within the South Devon AONB. The Inspector dismissed the appeal on the basis that the scale of the development in the context of the surrounding area constituted "major development":

> *"15. … As made clear in Annex 2/The Glossary and Footnote 70 to the Framework, for AONBs this does not mean development of 10 or more homes or a site with an area of 0.5 ha or more.*
>
> *16. However, in this instance, the proposal would involve a substantial extension of a very modest-sized settlement along the lower slopes of an unspoilt river valley.*
>
> *17. Moreover, the proposal would take place within a part of the landscape that is integral to the setting and charm of the village of Frogmore. It would comprise major development within the AONB."*

The Inspector also rejected a comparison with two other appeal decisions where larger schemes were held not to comprise major development because in both cases the existing settlements were towns and therefore the context for considering the scale of new development was very different:

> *"21. … Each case must be determined on its own merits and none of these other decisions set a precedent that I must follow."*

(c) APP/W0340/W/18/3211943, land off Charlotte Close, Hermitage, Berkshire (3 December 2018). In that case planning permission was sought for 36 dwellings with associated landscape and highway works within an AONB. The Inspector dismissed the appeal on the basis of the material harm that the scheme would cause to the AONB despite finding it would not amount to "major development":

> *"47. … I do not consider the appeal scheme to amount to major development in the sense of paragraph 172. In the context of a village of some 800 dwellings, it would not amount to a significant proportional increase (some 4.5%). While harm would be caused to the AONB as already discussed, it would be localised – being restricted to the site itself and a limited number of viewpoints. It would not therefore have a significant adverse impact in the terms set out in footnote 55. I note in this context that the Council does not consider either the Old Farmhouse scheme (21 units) or the site's development for the approximate 15 dwellings set out in policy HSA24 to amount to major development in this context. Nevertheless, this does not affect the material harm that the appeal scheme would cause to the AONB's natural beauty."*

3.21 It is thus difficult to draw any firm conclusions:

(a) In some post-footnote 55 appeals it is being recognised it was intended to define "major development" differently for purposes of para. 172 to that in the DMPO– the correct approach in our view;

(b) In some appeals Inspectors are taking the wrong approach and being unduly influenced by definition of "major development" for other purposes in the NPPF (2019) based on the DMPO and going on to say that it cannot be that major development means something "larger" in an AONB etc. – this is the wrong approach in our view;

(c) In some cases Inspectors are analysing matters on the facts, as under NPPF (2012), with little or no reference to the new NPPF and footnote 55[22].

### The major development test

3.22 The material parts of para. 172 of the NPPF are set out here for ease of reference

> *"Planning permission should be refused for major development other than in exceptional circumstances, and where it can be demonstrated that the development is in the public interest. Consideration of such applications should include an assessment of:*
> *(a) the need for the development, including in terms of any national considerations, and the impact of permitting it, or refusing it, upon the local economy;*
> *(b) the cost of, and scope for, developing outside the designated area, or meeting the need for it in some other way; and*

[22] See e.g. APP/M2270/W/18/3196553, APP/K1128/W/18/3205992, APP/X2220/W/18/3194604, APP/N2535/W/18/3200598, APP/X0415/W/18/3202036, APP/A2280/C/17/3177781 and APP/B9506/W/18/3196556.

> *(c) any detrimental effect on the environment, the landscape and recreational opportunities, and the extent to which that could be moderated."*

3.23 In an early case on the NPPF (2012), R (Mevagissey Parish Council) v Cornwall Council [2013] EWHC 3684 (Admin), Hickinbottom J (as he then was) considered the meaning of "exceptional circumstances" in the context of para. 116 of the NPPF (2012), the precursor to para. 172 of the NPPF (2019):

> *"7. … amongst material considerations, national policy gives the conservation of landscape and scenic beauty in an AONB a particular enhanced status. It requires an application for planning permission for a major development within an AONB to be refused, unless (i) there are exceptional circumstances ("exceptional" in this context connoting rarity); and (ii) it is demonstrated that, despite giving great weight to conserving the landscape and scenic beauty in the AONB, the development is in the public interest. As well as any detrimental effect of the development on the landscape, this national policy requires the planning decision-maker to assess, and take into consideration, the need for the development and the scope for meeting the assessed need in some other way.*
>
> …
>
> *51 Where an application is made for a development in an AONB, the relevant committee or other planning decision-makers are required to take into account and weigh all material considerations. However, as I have explained above (paragraph 6), the NPPF places the conservation of the landscape and scenic beauty of an AONB into a special category of material consideration: as a matter of policy paragraph 115 requires it to be given "great weight", and paragraph 116 of the NPPF requires permission for a major development such as this in an AONB to be refused*

> *save in exceptional circumstances and where it can be demonstrated the proposed development is in the public interest. In coming to a determination of such a planning application under this policy, the committee are therefore required, not simply to weigh all material considerations in a balance, but to refuse an application unless they are satisfied that (i) there are exceptional circumstances, and (ii) it is demonstrated that, despite giving great weight to conserving the landscape and scenic beauty in the AONB, the development is in the public interest … ".*

3.24 In Franks v SSCLG [2015] EWHC 3690 (Admin), Ouseley J stated at para. 29 "I am in agreement what Hickinbottom J held in R (Mevagissey Parish Council) v Cornwall Council [2013] EWHC 3684 (Admin), that paragraph 116 was one way, perhaps not the only way, ordained by the NPPF in which great weight could be given to the objective in paragraph 115 and therefore to any harm which a major development was assessed to do."

3.25 In SSCLG v Wealden DC [2018] Env LR, Lindblom LJ stated at para. 63:

> *"The policy requires the exercise of planning judgment. The decision-maker must consider whether there are "exceptional circumstances" justifying the granting of planning permission for the development in question, and whether granting permission would be "in the public interest". The three bullet points do not exclude other considerations relevant to those questions. The first requires the decision-maker to consider the "need for the development", including "any national considerations"—for example, the considerations of national policy for housing need and supply. The second bullet point does not refer specifically to alternative sites. It refers to the "cost" and "scope" for development "elsewhere outside the designated area", and to the possibility of meeting of the need for the development "in some other way". In many*

> *cases, this will involve the consideration of alternative sites. But the policy does not prescribe for the decision-maker how alternative sites are to be assessed in any particular case. It does not say that this exercise must relate to the whole of a local planning authority's administrative area, or to an area larger or smaller than that. This will always depend on the circumstances of the case in hand. The third bullet point requires the decision-maker to consider potential harm in the three respects referred to—again, always a matter of planning judgment."*

3.26 In the Wealden case the Inspector's conclusion that the para. 116 exceptionality/public interest test was met in relation to a scheme for 103 houses having regard to the extent of local need and the absence of alternatives was found to be lawful by the Court of Appeal.

3.27 The phrase "exceptional circumstances" also features in national policy on the Green Belt, in terms of the amendment of green belt boundaries in the course of a local plan process. In R (Luton BC) v Central Bedfordshire Council [2015] 2 P&CR 19, Sales LJ held at para. 54:

> *"The second sentence of para.83 of the NPPF provides guidance regarding the approach to be adopted if there is a proposal to alter the boundaries of the Green Belt in a local plan: exceptional circumstances have to be shown to justify such a course. But paras 87–88 of the NPPF provide guidance regarding the approach to be adopted if there is a proposal for development of an area within the Green Belt set out in a local plan: "very special circumstances" have to be shown. This is a stricter test than that in para.83 in respect of changing the boundaries of the Green Belt in the local plan."*

3.28 Policy on the amendment of boundaries of the Green Belt has been changed by amendments to the NPPF 2018. However, Luton BC does tend to suggest that the phrase "exceptional circumstances" alone is not the highest threshold in national planning policy; and see also the magisterial consideration of these matters in Compton Parish Council v Guildford BC [2020] J.P.L. 661 per Ouseley J[23]:

> *"68. There is no definition of the policy concept of "exceptional circumstances". This itself is a deliberate policy decision, demonstrating that there is a planning*

---

[23] There was an issue in that case on "major development" for AONB purposes:

> ***"Issue 6: The access road at Blackwell Farm and major development in the AONB***
> *209. NPPF [116] states:*
>
> > *"Planning permission should be refused for major developments in [AONB] except in exceptional circumstances and where it can be demonstrated they are in the public interest. Consideration of such applications should include an assessment of: the need for the development, including … the impact of permitting it, or refusing it, upon the local economy; the cost of, and scope for, developing elsewhere outside the designated area, or meeting the need for it in some other way; and any detrimental effect on the environment, the landscape and recreational opportunities, and the extent to which that could be moderated."*
> >
> > *The PPG, applicable with the 2012 NPPF, offered this help: whether or not a development was "major development" was for the decision-maker, taking into account the proposal and the local context. Great weight had to be given to conserving the landscape and scenic beauty of AONB, whether development was "major development" or not. The 2019 version of the NPPF added that the nature of a development, its scale, setting and the significance of its impact on the purposes of the designation as AONB were relevant. I do not read R. (on the application of JH and FW Green Ltd v South Downs National Park Authority [2018] EWHC 604 (Admin) at [27] as supporting a proposition that whether development was "major" should be determined solely by its degree of impact on the qualities of the AONB. That is obviously an important factor, and it may be decisive. But the PPG and 2019 version of the NPPF are correct in their approach to the meaning of "major development".*
> >
> > *211. It was not disputed but that NPPF [116] only applied in terms to development control decisions, but Mr Kimblin submitted that that did not mean that it had no ramifications in plan-making when assessing the deliverability of allocations. The soundness of the Plan required the allocations to be deliverable. The Inspector needed to recognise that Guildford BC or the Secretary of State might take the view that the access road was "major development" and conclude that the harm did not warrant the road or therefore the development allocation. Mr Kimblin pointed to the £20m cost of the link, what he described as the "very challenging topography" which the road had to cross; it was not simply a development access road but was intended to provide relief to the A31/A3 junction. (Perhaps this was an example of the wider benefits of the infrastructure brought by the allocations.) ..."*

*judgment to be made in all the circumstances of any particular case; Calverton Parish Council v Nottingham City Council [2015] EWHC 1078 at [20], Jay J. It is deliberately broad, and not susceptible to dictionary definition.*

*69. The parties agreed that whether a particular factor was capable of being an "exceptional circumstance" in any particular case was a matter of law; but whether in any particular case it was treated as such, was a matter of planning judgment. That does not take one very far, in my judgment, because a judicial decision that a factor relied on by a planning decision-maker as an "exceptional circumstance" was not in law capable of being one is likely to require some caution and judicial restraint. All that is required is that the circumstances relied on, taken together, rationally fit within the scope of "exceptional circumstances" in this context. The breadth of the phrase and the array of circumstances which may come within it place the judicial emphasis very much more on the rationality of the judgment than on providing a definition or criteria or characteristics for that which the policy-maker has left in deliberately broad terms.*

*70. "Exceptional circumstances" is a less demanding test than the development control test for permitting inappropriate development in the Green Belt, which requires "very special circumstances." That difference is clear enough from the language itself and the different contexts in which they appear, but if authority were necessary, it can be found in R(Luton BC) v Central Bedfordshire Council [2015] EWCA Civ 537 at [56], Sales LJ. As Patterson J pointed out in IM Properties Development Ltd v Lichfield DC [2014] EWHC 2240 at [90-91 and 95-96], there is no requirement that Green Belt land be released as a last resort, nor was it necessary to show that assumptions upon which the Green Belt boundary had been drawn, had been falsified by subsequent events.*

*71. There is however a danger of the simple question of whether there are "exceptional circumstances" being judicially over-analysed. This phrase does not require at least more than one individual "exceptional circumstance". The "exceptional circumstances" can be found in the accumulation or combination of circumstances, of varying natures, which entitle the decision-maker, in the rational exercise of a planning judgment, to say that the circumstances are sufficiently exceptional to warrant altering the Green Belt boundary.*

*72. General planning needs, such as ordinary housing, are not precluded from its scope; indeed, meeting such needs is often part of the judgment that "exceptional circumstances" exist; the phrase is not limited to some unusual form of housing, nor to a particular intensity of need. I accept that it is clearly implicit in the stage 2 process that restraint may mean that the OAN is not met. But that is not the same as saying that the unmet need is irrelevant to the existence of "exceptional circumstances", or that it cannot weigh heavily or decisively; it is simply not necessarily sufficient of itself. These factors do not exist in a vacuum or by themselves: there will almost inevitably be an analysis of the nature and degree of the need, allied to consideration of why the need cannot be met in locations which are sequentially preferable for such developments, an analysis of the impact on the functioning of the Green Belt and its purpose, and what other advantages the proposed locations, released from the Green Belt, might bring, for example, in terms of a sound spatial distribution strategy. The analysis in Calverton PC of how the issue should be approached was described by Jay J as perhaps a counsel of perfection; but it is not exhaustive or a checklist. The*

> *points may not all matter in any particular case, and others may be important especially the overall distribution of development, and the scope for other uses to be provided for along with sustainable infrastructure."*

3.29 Exceptional circumstances in the context of the amendment to Green Belt boundaries were considered by the Court of Appeal in Solihull MBC v Gallagher Estates Ltd [2015] JPL 714. At para. 36, Laws LJ held:

> *"The fact that a particular site within a council's area happens not to be suitable for housing development cannot be said without more to constitute an exceptional circumstance, justifying an alteration of the Green Belt by the allocation to it of the site in question. Whether development would be permitted on the sites concerned in this case, were they to remain outside the Green Belt, would depend upon the Council's assessment of the merits of any planning application put forward."*

3.30 Turning to some planning appeal decisions, again these are fact specific but give a flavour of how the test is applied:

(a) In Appeal APP/X0415/W/18/3202026, Old Red Lion, High Street, Great Missenden, HP16 0AU, the Inspector found that there were exceptional circumstances for residential development:

> *"I am satisfied that exceptional circumstances exist in this case, evidenced by the very limited scope for the provision of housing within Chiltern District on sites that do not lie within the AONB or the Green Belt; the fact that there is a severe shortfall against the housing requirement and that this shortfall has been persistent; and that the site lies in a sustainable location with easy access to local services and public transport, within one of the*

> *most sustainable settlements in the district. Indeed as this site has already been identified in the HELAA as being appropriate in principle for accommodating housing, it can reasonably be assumed that the council is satisfied that such development would not be at odds with CDLP Policy LSQ1 and the NPPF, and that it therefore accepts that exceptional circumstances exist."*

(b) In Appeal APP/Q3115/W/16/3165351 CABI International, Nosworthy Way, Mongewell, Wallingford, the Inspector considered policy on exceptional circumstances at para. 15 (footnote omitted):

> *"Paragraph 116 sets out three considerations in determining whether there are exceptional circumstances. The Wealden Court of Appeal decision made it clear that these are a matter of planning judgement but are not necessarily exclusive. A fair reading of the judgment in its context indicates that further considerations could comprise the benefits of the scheme. It did not suggest that harm, other than to the AONB, should be included in the assessment."*

The Inspector found that there were exceptional circumstances for the proposed development, being the erection of new headquarters for CABI, erection of 91 dwellings and associated works. At paras 40-41, the Inspector found:

> *"40 The scenic beauty of the AONB is determined by its special qualities. The site itself does not exhibit any of these, is a detractor in its present state and is likely to visually deteriorate further over time if the status quo is maintained. Furthermore, the intense screening along its*

*boundaries detaches its internal institutional character from the wider AONB. Any detrimental effects on the landscape arise from the external views and are primarily linked to the perception and experience of recreational users of the public rights of way as they travel through the designated countryside. For the reasons given above I consider that significant harm would arise in this respect and although it would diminish over time it would still be adverse and thus detrimental. In addition, there would be a small degree of harm to cultural heritage, which would thus not be conserved.*

*41 Section 85 of the Countryside and Rights of Way Act requires regard to be paid to the purpose of conserving and enhancing the natural beauty of the AONB. This is not the same thing as requiring that every development proposal engenders enhancement. Indeed if that were the case it is difficult to see how major development in an AONB could ever be permitted. It is clearly a matter of balance, but in undertaking that exercise the Framework makes clear that the conservation of the designated resource is a matter of great weight and Policy CSEN1 gives high priority to conservation and enhancement. The need for the development and the conclusion that there are presently no alternatives outside the designated area are also matters of substantial importance in the public interest. Improvements to biodiversity and the attractive appearance of the proposed new CABI building would be further positive factors in this case. Overall the benefits would outweigh the limited amount of harm that would be caused to the environment, landscape and recreational opportunities, in my judgement. For these reasons*

> *I conclude that in this particular case exceptional circumstances would be demonstrated."*

(c) In Appeal APP/D3125/W/16/3143885 Land south of High Street, Milton-under-Wychwood, an Inspector found that development for up to 62 dwellings would give rise to exceptional circumstances, stating at para. 43:

> *"With regard to para.116 of the NPPF the proposed development would have a positive effect on the local economy and there is no scope for developing to fulfil overall housing need in the Burford–Charlbury Sub Area outside the designated area. As concluded above the proposed development would have a less than significant effect on the character and visual amenity of the [AONB] and this effect would be moderated by proposed landscaping. The severe shortfall in housing land supply in the District and the need to deliver market and affordable housing in the Burford–Charlbury Sub Area that is almost wholly within the [AONB] combine to be the exceptional circumstances that justify major development of land in the [AONB]. Meeting housing need is, fundamentally, in the public interest."*

(d) In Appeal APP/U3935/V/14/2216792 Land at Science Museum, Wroughton, Swindon SN4 9LT, the Secretary of State granted permission for the installation of ground mounted photovoltaic solar arrays to provide 41 MW generation capacity with associated development. The Inspector noted the use of the site at para. 6 "The Science Museum… acquired the airfield to establish a primary storage facility. Stored at the Wroughton Object Storage facility re over 35,000 3D objects (generally all larger than a washing machine) and over 500,000 library and archive texts. Stored in the hangars are items such as large aircraft, printing presses, and the World's first hydrogen fuel car.". At para. 394, the Inspector held:

> *"If the income derived for the Science Museum from the proposed solar farm is used to enable the preservation of the many historic assets in their care then the proposed solar farm may be regarded to be enabling development. The Science Museum have stated, in an open forum, that the income derived would be ring-fenced for essential repairs, maintenance and upgrade of infrastructure and there is no reason to doubt that the income, if it ultimately derived, would be used for this purpose. Critics and objectors have accepted that there is no reason to suppose, particularly given that the Science Museum is a public body, that the income would be used for this purpose. It is undoubtedly the case that the improvements to infrastructure at the airfield that would flow from the proposed scheme would aid the preservation of the nation's heritage. This benefit of the scheme must be regarded to be in the public interest."*

The Inspector's conclusion on exceptional circumstances was at para. 399:

> *"In conclusion on exceptional circumstances small weight is given to ecological enhancements and, given that the Science Museum is seeking to enhance its ability to conserve heritage assets of national importance, weight is given to the income it would derive from the operation of the proposed solar farm."*

At para. 405, the Inspector stated:

> *"There is an identified need for the proposed solar farm at Wroughton airfield. This need is the generation of income for the Science Museum to contribute to its conservation of heritage assets of national importance. Objectors have been unable to counter the claim that the income could not be generated in any other way."*

At para. 407, the Inspector stated:

> *"With regard to paragraph 116 of the NPPF... exceptional circumstances exist in this case and these are clearly in the public interest. There is an identified need for the major development at the airfield and this need cannot be met by developing outside the AONB or in any other way. The circumstances of the Science Museum's need for the development are exceptional and outweigh the less than substantial harm that would be caused to the environment and the weight that is afforded to conservation of the landscape of the AONB. The proposed development accords with government policy on the natural environment."*

The Secretary of State stated at paras 15-17 of his decision:

> *"15. The Secretary of State also agrees with the Inspector (IR398-399) that, although there is no evidence to indicate that there would be any benefit to the local economy during the lifetime of the solar scheme, further ecological enhancements to the airfield would be achieved which would add an additional small benefit to the scheme.*
>
> *16. For the reasons given in IR400-405, the Secretary of State agrees with the Inspector's con-*

*clusions at IR406-407 that exceptional circumstances exist and outweigh the less than substantial harm which would be caused to the environment and the weigh afforded to conservation of the AONB. He also agrees with the Inspector's conclusion that there is an identified need which cannot be met by developing outside the AONB or in any other way, and that the proposed development would be in the public interest and in accordance with government policy on the natural environment.*

*17. The Secretary of State notes that it is agreed by all parties that the proposal would be a major development in the AONB and that paragraphs 115 and 116 of the Framework are therefore engaged. This is taken into account in his consideration of whether there are exceptional circumstances, which can also be demonstrated to be in the public interest, to justify the granting of planning permission."*

3.31 For other mostly earlier (and pre-NPPF) examples of major development proposals considered on appeal: see DCP online[24] at para 4.252. Examples of developments assessed on appeal or call-in under the major development test in NPs include: natural gas well and processing plant in the North York Moors NP, a military training area in Northumberland, an extension to a fluorspar quarry in the Peak District, a radioactive waste disposal facility in Cumbria.

3.32 The DCP also a useful discussion of appeal decisions in respect of renewable energy, telecommunications, tourist attractions, visitor accommodation, recreational facilities and local needs. In relation to AONBs the DCP considers a number of appeals that have applied the major development test including in respect of a

[24] www.dcp-online.co.uk – this is a subscription service.

trunk road in Kent, the Brighton & Hove Albion stadium, a solar farm in North Dorset, gravel workings in West Berkshire, a drilling facility in Kent, a motorway service area, a business park in the Dart Valley AONB, substations and pylons and the Longleat Centre Parcs.

## 4 OTHER ASPECTS OF PARAGRAPH 172

### Great weight to conserving and enhancing landscape and scenic beauty

4.1 It is important to bear in mind that the general admonition in para. 172 applies, even to development which does not constitute "major development", e.g. development inside a NP, the Broads or AONB but which is not categorised as "major". The decision-maker is still obliged to give "great weight" to conserving and enhancing landscape and scenic beauty in NPs, the Broads, and AONBs. As the Court made clear in Monkhill Ltd v Secretary of State for Housing, Communities and Local Government[25]:

> *"51. It is necessary to read the policy in paragraph 172 as a whole and in context. Paragraph 170 requires planning decisions to protect and enhance valued landscapes in a manner commensurate with their statutory status and any qualities identified in the development plan. Paragraph 172 points out that National Parks, the Broads and AONBs have "the highest status of protection" in relation to the conservation and enhancement of landscapes and scenic beauty. Not surprisingly, therefore, paragraph 172 requires "great weight" to be given to those matters. The clear and obvious implication is that if a proposal harms these objectives, great weight should be given to the decision-maker's assessment of the nature and degree of harm. The policy increases the weight to be given to that harm."*

[25] [2019] EWHC 1993 (Admin), [2020] PTSR 416

4.2 In Stroud DC v Secretary of State for Communities and Local Government [2015] EWHC 1940 (Admin). Ouseley J had to consider the NPPF (2012), and the application of policies on NPs the Broads and AONBs to development outside but nearby to these areas. His findings would, it seems to us, still apply to the revised policies in the NPPF (2019). He held (in what was an AONB case):

(a) Clearly from the wording the major development test only applied to development "in" an AONB;[26]

(b) In relation to what was then para. 115 of the NPPF (2012) and which provided "Great weight should be given to conserving landscape and scenic beauty in ... Areas of Outstanding Natural Beauty, which have the highest status of protection in relation to landscape and scenic beauty" (and is now part of para. 172 of the NPPF (2019)) that this "included the views from the AONB into the surrounding landscape, effectively taking the view that the beauty in the AONB would be harmed if looking out of it one saw ugliness"[27] and that "the Inspector would have been unrealistic in adopting so narrow a view as to ignore for the purposes of paragraph 115 views out of the AONB and the effect of development upon them";

(c) However, para.115 did not include "views into the AONB from outside". The Judge said "It seems to me that there is a very considerable distinction to be drawn between the two" (at [22]). The judge held:

> *"So the question is whether on the proper interpretation of paragraph 115 views of the AONB from outside the AONB fall within its scope. It is my judgment that that is not what policy 115 is intended to cover. It certainly covers the impact on*

---

26 At [5]

27 See paras [21] – [22]

> *the scenic beauty of the land actually within the AONB. It seems to me that it would be unduly restrictive to say that it could not cover the impact of land viewed in conjunction with the AONB from the AONB. But to go so far as to say that it must also cover land from which the AONB can be seen and great weight must be given to the conservation of beauty in the AONB by reference to that impact reads too much into paragraph 115. The effect of Miss Wigley's approach would be to give very widespread protection to land outside the AONB and not significant in views from the AONB. The Inspector noted that almost everywhere in Stroud District would fall into that category. That could not be, in my judgment, the correct interpretation of paragraph 115, and the word "in" If there was an error by the Inspector, it was an error against Mr Goatley rather than an error against Miss Wigley." (at [26])*

## Ecological factors

4.3 Applications for development in an AONB, NPs or the Broads are also subject to the provisions in para. 170 and 175 of the NPPF regarding the protection and enhancement of the natural environment. Paragraph 170 requires planning policies and decisions to contribute to, and enhance the natural environment by (inter alia) protecting and enhancing valued landscapes, sites of biodiversity or geological value and soils, and minimising impacts on, and providing net gains for biodiversity, including by "establishing coherent ecological networks that are more resilient to current and future pressures."[28] Para. 175 sets out that, in

[28] This policy objective is reflected in the draft Environment Bill, which was still being considered by the House of Commons when this Chapter was drafted. Clause 93 will, if enacted, amend s.40 of the Natural Environment and Rural Communities Act 2006 strengthening the duty to "conserve" biodiversity to a duty to "conserve and enhance" biodiversity. This is discussed further below at Chapter

determining planning applications, the local planning authority should apply a number of principles:

(a) If significant harm to biodiversity cannot be avoided, adequately mitigated or, as a last resort, compensated for, that planning permission should be refused;

(b) Development on land within, or outside an SSSI, and which is likely to have an adverse effect on it (individually or in combination with other developments) should not normally be permitted, the only exception being where the benefits of the proposed development "clearly outweigh" both its likely impacts on the features of the site for which it was designated and any broader impacts on the SSSI network;

(c) Development resulting in the loss or deterioration of irreplaceable habitats (such as ancient woodland) should be refused, unless there are "wholly exceptional reasons" and a suitable compensation strategy exists; and

(d) Development whose primary objective is to conserve or enhance biodiversity should be supported. Opportunities to incorporate biodiversity improvements should be encouraged.

4.4 Further guidance is provided in the NPPG.[29] Planning authorities are encouraged to work collaboratively with other partners, including Local Nature Partnerships, to develop and deliver a strategic approach to protecting and improving the natural environment.[30]

## Cultural heritage

5.

[29] 'Natural Environment'.

[30] Para.: 010 Reference ID: 8-010-20190721

4.5 Development in NPs, the Broads or AONBs involving or affecting heritage assets will need to consider the provisions of Chapter 16 of the NPPF[31] as well as the statutory duties under the Planning (Listed Buildings and Conservation Areas) Act.[32]

4.6 Para. 193 of the NPPF requires great weight to be given to an asset's conservation, when assessing the impacts of a proposed development on the significance of a heritage asset. Any harm to, or loss of, the significance of a designated heritage asset requires "clear and convincing justification" (para 194). Substantial harm to, or loss of, grade II listed buildings or grade II registered parks or gardens should be "exceptional" (para 194 (a)) Substantial harm to, or loss of, assets of the highest significance[33] should be "wholly exceptional" (para 194(b)).

4.7 Where a proposed development would lead to substantial harm to, or total loss of significance of, a designated heritage asset, consent should be refused unless it can be demonstrated that that harm, or loss, is "necessary to achieve substantial public benefits that outweigh that harm or loss" or the following criteria are satisfied:

a The nature of the heritage asset prevents all reasonable use of the site;

b No viable use of the heritage asset can be found in the medium term;

---

31 Further guidance is provided in the NPPG 'Historic Environment'

32 On which see generally, Steer v Secretary of State for Communities and Local Government [2018] EWCA Civ 1697 which provides a useful overview of the general principles and approach to identifying setting of a heritage asset.

33 i.e. scheduled monuments, protected wreck sites, registered battlefields, grade I and II* listed buildings, grade I and II* registered parks and gardens, and World Heritage Sites

c Conservation, through some form of grant funding or public, not for profit, or charitable ownership, is not possible; and

d The harm or loss is outweighed by the benefit of bringing the site back into use.[34]

4.8 Where the proposed development would lead to less than substantial harm to a designated heritage asset or its significance, then the harm should be weighed against the public benefit of the proposal, including, where appropriate, securing its "optimum viable use".[35]

4.9 Useful guidance on what is required of a decision maker considering an application for development in an AONB, close to a conservation area of historic interest that contained a listed building, was provided by the Planning Court in R (on the application of Advearse) v Dorset Council[36]:

> " *[...] As summarised above, what the Council was required to do was to assess the significance of the Conservation Area (and as the NPPF explained, the significance of the Conservation Area included its setting) and consider the extent of the impact of the proposed development on the significance of the Conservation Area. If, as in this case, the conclusion reached was that the proposed development would result in less than substantial harm to the Conservation Area then the Council needed to weigh that harm against the public benefits of the development. The Officer's Report does not address those matters in any coherent way. Even though what is*

---

34 Para. 195

35 On which, see R (on the application of JH and FW Gren Ltd) v South Downs National Park [2018] EWHC 604 (Admin) citing and applying R (Gibson) v Waverley Borough Council (No 1) [2012] EWHC 1472 (Admin) and R (Gibson) v Waverley Borough Council (No 2) [2015] EWHC 3784 (Admin).

36 [2020] EWHC 807 (Admin), per Swift J at paras and 2210

*required of an officer's report is not demanding, a report must meet some basic standards of good public administration. Planning decisions are entrusted to councillors because they are important local decisions. Planning issues are often controversial, all those affected by them deserve to be reassured that the officer's reports that inform councillor's decisions are sufficient to identify how any particular proposal is affected by specific statutory obligations which may apply (for example, the provisions of the Planning Listed Buildings Act said by Advearse to be material in this case), and by material policies such as those contained in Local Plans and the Secretary of State's NPPF.*

*21. Officer's reports must meet a basic level of coherence. No detailed legal exposition is required. In most instances any such approach will be best avoided. But if, as in this case, a relevant policy requires a particular matter to be addressed systematically, the report should include some narrative as to what the system is and how it applies to the case in hand. None of this is sophisticated. In this case, the Report needed to do no more than identify the conclusion as to the extent of the impact of the Vearse Farm Development and the reasons for that; explain that that harm needed to be assessed against the public benefits of the proposed developments; and then either state a reasoned conclusion on the matter or leave councillors to undertake the assessment for themselves."*

## Tranquillity

4.10 Para. 180 of the NPPF provides:

*"180. Planning policies and decisions should also ensure that new development is appropriate for its location taking into account the likely effects (including cumu-*

*lative effects) of pollution on health, living conditions and the natural environment, as well as the potential sensitivity of the site or the wider area to impacts that could arise from the development. In doing so they should:*

...

*b) identify and protect tranquil[37] areas which have remained relatively undisturbed by noise and are prized for their recreational and amenity value for this reason"*

4.11 Tranquillity is likely to be a key issue in NPs, the Broads and AONBs. The following appeal decisions illustrate some of the issues which may go beyond noise and encompass issues such as visual disturbance and "dark skies":

(a) The Secretary of State refused to grant permission for a waste water treatment works and sludge recycling centre at an existing works on the coast of what was the South Downs AONB because of the harm to the remoteness and tranquillity of the area: see APP/G1/440/A99/1026522;

(b) The conversion of a barn in the Yorkshire Dales NP to a bunkhouse able to accommodate thirteen tourists and holidaymakers was refused because it would lead to unacceptable levels of disturbance in a tranquil area of a valley, see APP/C9499/A/14/2212524;

---

37 See in the PPG:

*"What factors are relevant if seeking to identify areas of tranquillity?*
*For an area to justify being protected for its tranquillity, it is likely to be relatively undisturbed by noise from human sources that undermine the intrinsic character of the area. It may, for example, provide a sense of peace and quiet or a positive soundscape where natural sounds such as birdsong or flowing water are more prominent than background noise, e.g. from transport.*

*Consideration may be given to how existing areas of tranquility could be further enhanced through specific improvements in soundscape, landscape design (e.g. through the provision of green infrastructure) and/or access.*
*Para.: 008 Reference ID: 30-008-20190722*
*Revision date: 22 07 2019"*

(c) Two wind turbines located three to four kilometres outside a national park were also judged to harm its setting, see APP/N6845/A/13/220983. The open landscape with extensive views towards mountain ranges was sensitive to the introduction of even one turbine, and tranquillity would be diminished by the movement of the blades;

(d) In APP/L3815/A/02/1098439 an inspector was concerned that increasing facilities and accommodation at a Children's Recreation & Study Centre would result in increased noise and disturbance to the detriment of the remote and tranquil nature of the AONB. In reaching this decision, the inspector noted that although there were benefits associated with increasing enjoyment of the countryside, the aim of protecting the AONB was paramount;

(e) However, an Inspector permitted the retention of a moto-cross site in the South Downs NP and East Hampshire AONB. He found that there was a need for the facility and that while two events a year would have some impact on the tranquillity of the area, it was not unusual for large events to take place in a rural area particularly in the late summer months, see APP/L1765/A/09/2113799.

4.12 The CPRE hosts a number of resources on tranquillity: see e.g. https://www.cpre.org.uk/resources/tranquility-map-england/ and https://www.cpre.org.uk/wp-content/uploads/2019/11/tranquillity_mapping_developing_a_robust_methodology_for_planning_support.pdf.

4.13 See also the approach taken in the South Downs National Park Tranquillity Study which provides the following explanation:[38]

> *"What is Tranquillity?*

[38] https://www.southdowns.gov.uk/wp-content/uploads/2017/03/13-04-17-South-Downs-National-Park-Tranquillity-Study.pdf

*1.1 Tranquillity is considered to be a state of calm, quietude and is associated with a feeling of peace. It relates to quality of life, and there is good scientific evidence that it also helps to promote health and well-being. It is a perceptual quality of the landscape, and is influenced by things that people can both see and hear in the landscape around them.*

*Why did we set out to map areas of Tranquillity within the National Park?*

*1.2 'Tranquil and unspoilt places' are one of seven special qualities of the National Park. They are the key characteristics that help make this place special. As a special quality of the National Park, it is something that visitors and residents greatly value. In many areas of the National Park, the landscape largely lacks intrusive development and retains areas of dark night sky. In a busy and pressured area like the South East of England these qualities are especially important.*

*1.3 These are not characteristics that apply uniformly across the whole of the National Park. Some areas are more tranquil then others, dependent on a wide number of influences. To date it has been difficult to properly identify areas that have the greatest, or least, tranquillity.*

*1.4 The tranquillity mapping project is a means for us to be able to do this and is intended as evidence work for our Local Plan*[39]*. Once we have completed the work we*

---

39 See Policy SD7 in the adopted SDNPA Local Plan

"Strategic Policy SD7: Relative Tranquillity

1. Development proposals will only be permitted where they conserve and enhance relative tranquillity and should consider the following impacts:

a) Direct impacts that the proposals are likely to cause by changes in the visual and aural environment in the immediate vicinity of the proposals;

b) Indirect impacts that may be caused within the National Park that are remote from the location of the proposals themselves such as vehicular movements; and

> *will be able to use the results across a wide range of our activities – including in relation to our planning work. It is our intention to use the data we collect to help protect and enhance areas of high tranquillity within the National Park*"

## Navigation in the Broads

4.14 In addition to its role as local planning authority, one of the Broad's statutory purposes is to protect the interests of navigation on the waterways. Policy SP13 of the Local Plan for the Broads 2015-2036 makes specific provision in respect of navigable water space, and provides (inter alia) that navigable water space will be protected and enhanced through "avoiding development and changes in land management which are detrimental to its use".[40] Policies DM31 and DM32 address developments that encourage and support the use of the waterways and riverbank stabilisation respectively, subject to the need to ensure safe navigation / that development will not adversely impact navigation. The Broads Authority must take any authorisation or enforcement decision in accordance with the UK Marine Policy Statement[41] and the relevant Marine Plan – the East Inshore and Offshore Marine Plans 2014[42] – or state its reasons for not doing so.[43]

---

c) Experience of users of the PRoW network and other publicly accessible locations.

2. Development proposals in highly tranquil and intermediate tranquillity areas should conserve and enhance, and not cause harm to, relative tranquillity.

3. Development proposals in poor tranquillity areas should take opportunities to enhance relative tranquillity where these exist."

40 https://www.broads-authority.gov.uk/__data/assets/pdf_file/0036/259596/Local-Plan-for-the-Broads.pdf

41 https://assets.publishing.service.gov.uk/government/uploads/system/uploads/attachment_data/file/69322/pb3654-marine-policy-statement-110316.pdf.

42 https://www.gov.uk/government/collections/east-marine-plans

43 S.58 of the Marine and Coastal Access Act 2009

## 5 THE PRESUMPTION IN FAVOUR OF SUSTAINABLE DEVELOPMENT

5.1 The presumption in favour of sustainable development is the 'golden thread' running through the NPPF (2019).[44] Para 11 of the NPPF sets out that plans and decision making should apply a presumption in favour of sustainable development. For decision-making, the NPPF states that this means:

> *"(c) Approving development proposals that accord with an up-to-date development plan without delay; or*
>
> *(d) When there are no relevant development plan policies, or the policies which are the most important for determining the application are out-of-date, granting permission unless*
>
>> *i The application of policies in the NPPF that protect areas or assets of particular importance provides a clear reason for refusing the development proposed [fn6]; or*
>>
>> *ii Any adverse impacts of doing so would significantly and demonstrably outweigh the benefit, when assessed against the policies in this Framework, taken as a whole."*

5.2 Fn 6 is important in this context. This states that:

> *"The policies referred to are those in this Framework (rather than those in development plans) relating to: habitats sites (and those sites listed in paragraph 176) and/or designated as Sites of Special Scientific Interest; land designated as Green Belt, Local Green Space, an Area of Outstanding Natural Beauty, a National Park (or within the Broads Authority) or defined as Heritage*

44 Albeit, no longer expressly so.

> *Coast; irreplaceable habitats; designated heritage assets (and other heritage assets of archaeological interest referred to in footnote 63); and areas at risk of flooding or coastal change."*

5.3 A survey of, or even attempt to summarise, the copious case law which the para. 11 and footnote 6[45] have given rise to is beyond the scope of this text. What is material for the purposes of this text, however, is that where there are no relevant development plan policies, or those most important for determining the application are out of date, the 'tilted balance' in para. 11(d)(ii) is not engaged if the development would conflict with policies in the NPPF relating to AONBs, a NP, or the Broads Authority. This includes where the proposed development would not accord with para. 172 of the NPPF – even where it does not constitute major development. That was conclusion reached by Holgate J in Monkhill[46], holding that the first part of para. 172 of the NPPF is capable of sustaining a clear and independent reason for refusal of a planning application such as to prevent the application of the tilted balance.[47] As the Judge stated at paras. 52-3:

> *" Plainly, in a simple case where there would be harm to an AONB but no countervailing benefits, and therefore no balance to be struck between "pros and cons", the effect of giving great weight to what might otherwise be assessed as a relatively modest degree of harm, might be sufficient as a matter of planning judgment to amount to a reason for refusal of planning permission, when, absent that policy, that might not be the case. But where there are also countervailing benefits, it is self-evident that the issue for the decision-maker is whether those benefits outweigh the harm assessed, the significance of the latter being increased by the requirement to give "great weight"*

---

45 And/or their predecessors in earlier versions of the NPPF

46 See above.

47 See paras. 42-62.

*to it. This connotes a simple planning balance which is so obvious that there is no interpretive or other legal requirement for it to be mentioned expressly in the policy. It is necessarily implicit in the application of the policy and a matter of planning judgment. The "great weight" to be attached to the assessed harm to an AONB is capable of being outweighed by the benefits of a proposal, so as to overcome what would otherwise be a reason for refusal.*

*53. Interpreted in that straight forward, practical way, the first part of paragraph 172 of the NPPF is capable of sustaining a clear reason for refusal, whether in the context of paragraph 11(d)(i) or, more typically where that provision is not engaged, in the general exercise of development management powers."*

5.4 This decision is (at the time of writing) under appeal.

## 6 OTHER RELEVANT GUIDANCE: THE PPG AND THE NP CIRCULAR

6.1 Further guidance on development in AONBs, NPs and the Broads is contained in the NPPG – "Natural Environment"[48] – and NP Circular.[49] There is no equivalent circular for AONBs, but guidance is available on Natural England's website.[50] It is also necessary to briefly mention National Policy Statements under the Planning Act 2008.

---

48 Reference ID: 8-038-20190721 paras. 038 – 042.

49 https://assets.publishing.service.gov.uk/government/uploads/system/uploads/attachment_data/file/221086/pb13387-vision-circular2010.pdf

50 https://www.gov.uk/guidance/areas-of-outstanding-natural-beauty-aonbs-designation-and-management

## The PPG

6.2 By way of summary, the PPG sets out the statutory duties which apply to local planning authorities in relation to NPs, the Broads and AONBs, and how development in, or affecting the setting of those areas, should be approached. In respect of development within NPs, the Broads and AONBs, it identifies that the NPPF policies may mean it is not possible to meet objectively assessed needs for development in full through the plan-making process – and that they are unlikely to be suitable areas for meeting unmet need from adjoining areas. The need for effective joint working with neighbouring authorities is therefore of particular importance.

6.3 In terms of development outside, but potentially affecting the setting of NPs, AONBs and the Broads, the PPG identifies that land within the setting of those areas "often makes an important contribution to maintaining their natural beauty", that poorly located or designed development can do "significant harm", and that development within the setting of those area therefore requires "sensitive handling" that takes those potential impacts into account.

## *English National Parks and the Broads: UK Government Vision and Circular 2010* ("the NP Circular")

6.4 The NP Circular sets out a vision for English NPs and the Broads, setting out the aspiration that by 2030 they will be places with thriving, living, working landscapes notable for their natural beauty and cultural heritage; where sustainable development can be seen in action; where wildlife flourishes and habitats are maintained, restored, expanded and linked to other ecological networks, and "everyone can discover the rich variety of England's natural and historic environment".[51] The NP Circular identifies priority outcomes for 2010-15 with suggested actions,[52]

[51] Chapter 3

[52] Chapter 4

provides guidance on key legislative requirements and functions of authorities,[53] and guidance on relationships with other stakeholders such as Natural England.

6.5 The NP Circular also provides specific guidance on NP Management Plans and the Broads Plan;[54] Planning responsibilities (and documents to which the authorities must have regard);[55]Mineral Working in Parks,[56] biodiversity;[57] and access to open country and the coast under CROW 2000.[58]

## National Policy Statements

6.6 It is beyond the scope of this book to set out the provisions that deal with National Policy Statements under the 2008 Act. However, it should be noted that NPS EN-1 (which also applies in Wales) provides this guidance:

> *"Development proposed within nationally designated landscapes*
>
> *5.9.9 National Parks, the Broads and AONBs have been confirmed by the Government as having the highest status of protection in relation to landscape and scenic beauty. Each of these designated areas has specific statutory purposes which help ensure their continued protection and which the IPC should have regard to in its decisions. The conservation of the natural beauty of the landscape and countryside should be given substantial weight by the IPC in deciding on applications for development consent in these areas.*

[53] Chapter 5

[54] Chapter 5.1

[55] Chapter 5.2

[56] Chapter 5.3

[57] Chapter 5.9

[58] Chapter 5.10. See also Chapter 8 of this book

> *5.9.10 Nevertheless, the IPC may grant development consent in these areas in exceptional circumstances. The development should be demonstrated to be in the public interest and consideration of such applications should include an assessment of:*
>
> • *the need for the development, including in terms of national considerations, and the impact of consenting or not consenting it upon the local economy;*
>
> • *the cost of, and scope for, developing elsewhere outside the designated area or meeting the need for it in some other way, taking account of the policy on alternatives set out in Section 4.4; and*
>
> • *any detrimental effect on the environment, the landscape and recreational opportunities, and the extent to which that could be moderated.*
>
> *5.9.11 The IPC should ensure that any projects consented in these designated areas should be carried out to high environmental standards, including through the application of appropriate requirements where necessary."*

## 7 PLANNING POLICY IN WALES ON NATIONAL PARKS AND AONBs

7.1 Para 6.32 of Planning Policy Wales ("PPW") says that "The landscapes of Wales are rich and varied. Many Welsh landscapes are iconic, and a quarter of the land area of Wales is designated as either a National Park or Area of National Outstanding Beauty (AONB)[59]. The character and special qualities of all our places and landscapes, both urban and rural, can provide a strong sense

---

[59] See https://www.visitwales.com/things-do/nature-landscapes/national-parks: 20% of Wales is made up of land designated as a NP.

of place, inspiration and belonging, and contribute to the distinctive cultural identity of Wales".

7.2 The national policy context in Wales for NPs and AONBs has some similarities to but also a number of differences with the position in England. Thus, PPW provides that:

> ***"National Parks and Areas of Outstanding Natural Beauty***
> *6.3.5 The statutory landscape designations that apply in Wales are National Parks, and AONBs. Planning authorities have a statutory duty to have regard to National Parks and AONB purposes.*
> *This duty applies in relation to all activities affecting National Parks and AONBs, whether those activities lie within, or in the setting of, the designated areas. The designated landscapes should be drivers of the sustainable use and management of natural resources in their areas, and planning authorities should have regard to their identified special qualities in the exercise of their functions and any relevant management plans.*
> *6.3.6 In National Parks, planning authorities should give great weight to the statutory purposes of National Parks, which are to conserve and enhance their natural beauty, wildlife and cultural heritage, and to promote opportunities for public understanding and enjoyment of their special qualities. Planning authorities should also seek to foster the social, economic and cultural well-being of their local communities.*
> *6.3.7 In AONBs, planning authorities should give great weight to conserving and enhancing the natural beauty of AONBs, and should have regard to the wildlife, cultural heritage and social and economic well-being of the areas.*
> *6.3.8 National Parks and AONBs are of equal status in terms of landscape and scenic beauty, and must both be afforded the highest status of protection from inappropriate developments.*

> *6.3.9 The special qualities of designated areas should be given weight in the development planning and the development management process. Proposals in National Parks and AONBs must be carefully assessed to ensure that their effects on those features which the designation is intended to protect are acceptable. The contribution that development makes to the sustainable management of the designated area must be considered.*
>
> *6.3.10 In National Parks or AONBs, special considerations apply to major development proposals which are more national than local in character. Major developments should not take place in National Parks or AONBs except in exceptional circumstances. This may arise where after rigorous examination, there is demonstrated to be an overriding public need, refusal would be severely detrimental to the local economy and there is no potential for locating the development elsewhere or meeting the need in some other way. Any construction and restoration must be carried out to high environmental standards. Consideration of applications for major developments should therefore include an assessment of:*
>
> - *the need for the development, in terms of national considerations and the impact of permitting it or refusing it upon the local economy;*
> - *the cost of and scope for providing the development outside the designated area or meeting the need for it in some other way; and*
> - *any detrimental effect on the environment and the landscape, and the extent to which that could be moderated and/or mitigated."*

7.3 The differences include the following:

(a) the fact that in Wales "major development" is referred to as "major development proposals which are more national than local in character". This might suggest a narrower definition of what constitutes "major development" in Wales as opposed to England, because in England a development does not need to be more national than local to be major, see for example the 103 houses proposed in the ***Wealden*** case discussed in Chapter 4. The effect may thus be that fewer developments will be categorised as "major development" in Wales. Earlier versions of the PPW were in similar form, as indeed was PPG7 in England (see e.g. the discussion in ***Lake District Special Planning Board v British Nuclear Fuels plc*** (1993) 8 P.A.D. 311)[60]. The difference between Welsh and English definitions of major development was considered by the Welsh Ministers and the Inspector in an appeal concerning the re-development of a former army camp at Cwrt Y Gollen, near Crickhowell (dated 2 November 2011). The difference was apparent at that time even as between PPW and PPS7. The Inspector noted that the different approaches meant that the definition of major developments was materially broader in England (see para. 229). The Inspector said that Ministers should consider the matter (see para. 233). The Welsh Ministers gave the point short shrift saying that as planning was a devolved matter they were entitled to take a different view. This raises some potentially interesting issues in the Wye Valley AONB which straddles England and Wales, and where different definitions of what is "major development" will apply as will different policy wording. The suggestion by the Welsh Ministers in the Cwrt Y Gollen decision is that these differences are deliberate. The differences have grown with the NPPF. It is hard to accept though that these differences are the result of anything more than an inad-

60 This exposes a concern that arises with the position in England. Where development is determined to be major in England despite not being national in character it may not be easy to meet the exceptional circumstances test;

vertent failure in Wales to update the policies from PPG7 days;

(b) The definition of "major development" introduced in England in the NPPF (2018) (see Chapter 4) does not apply in Wales;

(c) The requirement for "rigorous examination" of whether there are exceptional circumstances for major development proposals was included in PPS7 but is now absent from the NPPF, it remains part of the PPW;

(d) On exceptional circumstances test the NPPF says "in exceptional circumstances, and where it can be demonstrated that the development is in the public interest". The PPW: says this re exceptional circumstances: (i) exceptional circumstances may be demonstrated "if there is "an overriding public need" – note the language is different "in the public interest" (England) as against "overriding public need" (Wales); (ii) the PPW in the main text of the policy repeats two matters set out in the 3 criteria so (i) impact on local economy and (ii) alternatives.

(e) On the 3 criteria to be considered: the same except that on the 3rd in England says "any detrimental effect on the environment, the landscape <u>and recreational opportunities</u>, and the extent to which that could be moderated" – underlined words not in PPW.

7.4 The PPW also provides that "Minerals development should not take place in National Parks and AONB except in very exceptional circumstances" (see para 5.14.35). It also provides that "Minerals development proposed adjacent or close to a National Park or AONB that might affect the setting of these areas, should be assessed carefully to determine whether the environmental and amenity impact is acceptable or not, or whether suitable, satisfactory conditions can be imposed to mitigate the impact" (see para 5.14.36). Mineral land banking requirements are also disapplied in AONBs and NPs (see para. 5.14.15). In a called-in decision concerning a proposed phased 8.33ha extension to a 12.4ha sand and gravel quarry with a recently expired planning permission and proposed 1.1 million extraction at Pant Gynn Quarry (3 August 2010) the Welsh Ministers in granting permission it was determined that while there was no obligation to have a landbank within a national park, a shortfall in landbank, although significant, should not by itself be an exceptional circumstance to permit major development but in combination with benefits to the rural economy, compliance with the development plan, a lack of statutory consultee objections and restoration benefits was enough to establish exceptional circumstances. See also the called-in decision in respect of Trefigin Quarry (4 October 2011).

7.5 In Wales, a similar circular to the NP Circular was published in 2007. This was called *Working Together for Wales: Policy Statement for the National Parks and National Park Authorities in Wales.* It does not cover major development and places more emphasis on the local community, community engagement and the local economy. However, this Circular has likely been overtaken by the Welsh Government's more recent publication *Valued and Resilient: The Welsh Government's Priorities for Areas of Outstanding Natural Beauty and National Parks* (July 2018).[61]

## 8 CASE-LAW IN RELATION TO WALES

8.1 In Council for National Parks Ltd v Pembrokeshire Coast National Park Authority [2005] EWCA Civ 888 the Court of Appeal upheld a decision to grant a major development in a National Park despite an officer recommendation for refusal. The case concerned the Bluestone Holiday Village ("Bluestone"), which was on a 200-hectare site. Factors upheld as relevant to the

[61] https://gov.wales/sites/default/files/publications/2019-04/areas-outstanding-natural-beauty-national-parks-2018-report%20.pdf

decision included that: (i) that the PPW allowed consideration of "the impact of permitting it or refusing it upon the local economy" in assessing major development and that the same factors were also relevant as a result of s. 11A of the 1949 Act; (ii) the policy is less stringent than Green Belt Policy and permits major development schemes within the National Park "in exceptional circumstances"; and (iii) there were other relevant factors "including the proximity of the site to the edge of the National Park and to the Oakwood development which lies beyond its boundary. Our attention was also drawn to the landscaping features of the proposed development".

8.2 The following are examples of major development considered on appeals, call-ins, DCO or Electricity Act 1989 applications on the basis of exceptional circumstances in Wales:

(a) Very large quarry extensions: see above;

(b) A combined heat and power ("CHP") plant near a village in the Pembrokeshire coast national park was granted a development consent order by the secretary of State for Energy and climate change ("SSfEC"), who found that national need and the local economic benefits the development would bring were not outweighed by its potential adverse impacts (the South Hook CHP Order, 23 October 2014). This was based on national need, local economic benefits and the proposed mitigation;

(c) A biomass fuelled generation station at Penrhos Works, Holyhead, Anglesey (4 April 2014) was granted S. 36 Electricity Consent a and direction under s. 90(2) of the TCPA 1990 for deemed PP granted by SSfECC. The site located just within the Ynys Mon/Anglesey AONB. It was found that there was an overriding need for project. Local employment opportunities emphasised. The view was taken that the need and the benefits to local economy outweighed disbenefits. There was said to be no suitable alternative elsewhere on Anglesey would have less impact on AONB and that planning conditions would help mitigate impacts on the AONB

(d) An application under the Electricity Act 1989 for 17 x 126m wind turbines located within an AONB area of high sensitivity to turbines of the scale proposed was refused. The Secretary of State accepted the renewable energy benefits however the scale of the landscape and visual effect impacts, the impacts on residential amenity and the detraction from the historic character of the landscape would be in conflict with the relevant provisions of Energy National Policy Statements, Welsh Government policies and local development plan policies. The proposal would affect 44 percent of an AONB, substantially harming its character while the experience of many residents of a residential scatter would be of living within or on the edge of a wind farm landscape dominated by large scale turbines. As a prominent modern feature the proposal would cause less than substantial harm to the onsite and surrounding historic features (decision 7 September 2015, land in Powys, Mid-Wales (Llandbadarn Fynydd). And see also the decision under the same Act in respect of land in Powys, Mid-Wales (Lllaithddu) for two groups of wind turbines with 1.5km separating gap in a high upland plateau with an installed total capacity of 62MW. Proposal 1 of 6 schemes. a) 12 x 115m turbines and b) 15 x 99.5m turbine (7 September 2015).

8.3 For cases considering the impacts of development close to but not within National Parks in Wales: see the decisions in respect of a and in Powys, Mid-Wales (Llandinam Repowering) (7 September 2015, close to the Snowdonia National Park) and see also land in Powys, Mid-Wales (Llanbrynmair) (same date), the Llandinam Wind Farm to Welshpool Substation in Powys, Mid Wales (same date) and land in Powys, Mid-Wales (Carnedd Wen) (same date). In the latter the Secretary of State in allowing the scheme gave less weight to views out of the National Park towards the turbines than did the Inspector.

## 9 PLANNING POLICY IN NORTHERN IRELAND REGARDING AONBs

9.1 As noted in Chapter 1 Northern Ireland does not have any national parks but it does have 8 AONBs (Antrim Coast and Glens AONB, Binevenagh AONB, Causeway Coast AONB, Lagan Valley AONB, Mourne AONB, Ring of Gullion AONB, Shared Horizons, Sperrin AONB and Strangford and Lecale AONB.

9.2 Planning Policy Statement 2 Natural Heritage provides so far as relevant (at para 2.15):

(a) "Under the Nature Conservation and Amenity Lands (Northern Ireland) Order 1985, other statutory designations include ... Areas of Outstanding Natural Beauty – designated by the Department primarily for their high landscape quality, wildlife importance and rich cultural and architectural heritage. The Department can also designate a National Park under this legislation";

(b) Policy NH 6 deals with Areas of Outstanding Natural Beauty and provides:

> *"Planning permission for new development within an Area of Outstanding Natural Beauty will only be granted where it is of an appropriate design, size and scale for the locality and all the following criteria are met:*
>
> *a) the siting and scale of the proposal is sympathetic to the special character of the Area of Outstanding Natural Beauty in general and of the particular locality; and*

> *b) it respects or conserves features (including buildings and other man-made features) of importance to the character, appearance or heritage of the landscape; and*
> *c) the proposal respects:*
> *local architectural styles and patterns;*
> *traditional boundary details, by retaining features such as hedges, walls, trees and gates; and local materials, design and colour."*

(c) The supporting text explains that "[t]his policy requires development proposals in Areas of Outstanding Natural Beauty (AONB) to be sensitive to the distinctive special character of the area and the quality of their landscape, heritage and wildlife" (see para. 5.14) and that "[t]he quality, character and heritage value of the landscape of an AONB lies in their tranquillity, cultural associations, distinctiveness, conservation interest, visual appeal and amenity value" (see para. 5.15). It is also advised (see para. 5.16) that "[i]n assessing proposals account will be taken of the Landscape Character Assessments and any other published guidance such as countryside assessments produced as part of the development plan process, as well as AONB Management Plans and local design guides" and that "[t]he Countryside Assessments will consider each designated AONB to identify each local landscape character type and their potential for protection and enhancement" (see para. 5.17).

(d) The Strategic Planning Policy Statement for Northern Ireland (2015) ("SPSS") states at paragraph 6.187 that development proposals in AONBs must be sensitive to the distinctive special character of the area and the quality of the landscape, heritage and wildlife. Paragraph 6.188 provides that in assessing proposals, including cumulative impacts in such areas, account will also be taken of the Landscape Character Assessments and any other relevant guidance including AONB management plans.

(e) The explanatory text at paragraphs 5.14 and 5.16 is identical to that in paragraphs 6.187 and 6.188 of the SPPS: see further Chapter 3 of this book.

9.3 Further information on the Northern Irish AONBs can be found at https://www.daera-ni.gov.uk/topics/land-and-landscapes/areas-outstanding-natural-beauty.

## 10 CASE-LAW REGARDING AONBS IN NORTHERN IRELAND

10.1 There are examples of cases before the Northern Irish Courts which have involved development in AONBs: see e.g. Quinn, Re Judicial Review [2013] NIQB 24 (22 February 2013) (refusal on appeal of energy wind-farm in the Sperrins AONB quashed but on non AONB grounds); Causeway Coast, Re Judicial Review [2019] NIQB 34 (unsuccessful judicial review of planning permission in the Causeway Coast AONB). There is though little or no exposition of the legal issues involved with AONBs in any of these cases.

# CHAPTER FOUR ANNEX

## Unit Numbers and Major Development: Examples

| Appeal number | Date | Units | Major Development? |
|---|---|---|---|
| APP/R3650/A/14/2223115 | 19/05/2015 | 5 | No |
| APP/K1128/W/18/3205992 | 27/12/2018 | 8 | No |
| APP/P0119/W/18/3217157 | 27/06/2019 | 8 | No |
| APP/Y9507/A/14/2220580 | 17/03/2015 | 10 | No |
| APP/Q1153/W/16/3157958 | 13/12/2016 | 10 | Yes (0.7 ha site) |
| APP/W0340/W/18/3211943 | 15/02/2019 | 11 | No |
| APP/M2270/W/18/3196553 | 18/01/2019 | 12 | No |
| APP/P1615/A/13/2204158 | 23/06/2014 | 15 | Yes |
| APP/K1128/W/18/3218669 | 13/06/2019 | 18 | No |
| APP/D0840/W/16/3146313 | 01/11/2016 | 20 | Yes |
| APP/E2734/W/16/3157795 | 16/12/2016 | 20 | Yes |
| APP/F1230/W/16/3156531 | 11/08/2017 | 20 | No |
| APP/D0840/W/18/3208554<br>APP/D0840/W/18/3213658 | 07/03/2019 | 20 | Yes |
| APP/Q1153/W/17/3177360 | 06/02/2018 | 22 | No |
| APP/U1430/W/17/3184449 | 08/02/2018 | 24 | No |
| APP/K1128/W/18/3208541 | 26/03/2019 | 24 | Yes |
| APP/D3830/A/14/2211981 | 02/03/2015 | 25 | No |
| APP/C1625/W/17/3175953 | 31/01/2018 | 25 | No |
| APP/Y9507/A/14/2218678 | 30/10/2014 | 26 | Yes |
| APP/U1105/W/15/3032502 | 23/12/2015 | 26 | Yes |

| | | | |
|---|---|---|---|
| APP/B1225/W/16/3162354 | 28/03/2017 | 28 | No |
| APP/K1128/W/17/3185418 | 17/08/2018 | 28 | Yes |
| APP/W1850/W/17/3172427 | 13/12/2017 | 29 | Yes |
| APP/Y2736/A/13/2197184 | 13/11/2013 | 30 | No |
| APP/Y9507/A/13/2204544 | 13/03/2014 | 30 | No |
| APP/X1118/W/15/3012049 | 11/04/2016 | 30 | No |
| APP/F1610/W/16/3165805 | 02/11/2017 | 30 | No |
| APP/X0415/W/18/3202036 | 04/09/2018 | 30 | No |
| APP/K1128/W/16/3156062 | 05/06/2017 | 32 | No |
| APP/G1630/W/17/3171926 | 05/10/2017 | 35 | No |
| APP/N2535/W/18/3200598 | 24/10/2018 | 35 | Yes (unreasoned) |
| APP/W0340/W/18/3200575 | 03/12/2018 | 36 | No |
| APP/G1630/W/15/31389514 | 20/09/2016 | 38 | No |
| APP/V3120/W/16/3153209 | 04/11/2016 | 40 | Yes |
| APP/B9506/W/18/3196556 | 24/08/2018 | 41 | Yes |
| APP/J3530/W/17/3172629 | 21/11/2018 | 43 | Yes |
| APP/U1105/A/14/2211701 | 11/06/2014 | 46 | Yes |
| APP/Z3825/W/15/3130269 | 22/02/2016 | 48 | Yes |
| APP/D3125/W/18/3209551 | 21/06/2019 | 68 | Yes |
| APP/D3830/A/13/2198213 | 01/05/2014 | 75-90 | Yes |

# CHAPTER FIVE

# WILDLIFE AND BIODIVERSITY ISSUES IN NATIONAL PARKS

*Stephen Whale and James Neill*

## 1. INTRODUCTION

1.1 This chapter examines the legal issues surrounding the protection and management of wildlife and biodiversity in NPs.

1.2 Chapter 1 explained how the key statutory purpose of conserving and enhancing natural beauty under section 5(1) of the 1949 Act includes the preservation of its "flora, fauna, geological and physiographical features" by virtue of sub-section 114(2) of the Act. It also set out how, when deciding whether to designate a NP, Natural England must "take into account its wildlife heritage": section 5(2A) of the 1949 Act, and how the Sandford Principle (implemented by section 11A(2) of the 1949 Act) requires greater weight to be attached "to the purpose of enhancing the natural beauty, wildlife and cultural heritage" of a NP. Thus nature conservation lies at the heart of the purposes and function of a NP.

1.3 Section 65(5) of the EA 1995 confers broad powers on NPAs to do anything which, in the opinion of that authority, is calculated to facilitate, or is conducive or incidental to, the accomplishment of those purposes. It also sets out at Schedule 8 a series of supplemental and incidental powers, and Schedule 9 sets out various miscellaneous provisions. This chapter explores in more detail the specific nature conservation powers which are available to NPs under those schedules, and how those powers relate to similar powers conferred on other statutory bodies, in particular (in England) Natural England and (in Wales) the NRBW. It also examines how nature conservation and biodiversity issues are considered as part of an NPA's planning function.

## 2 NATURE RESERVES

2.1 NPAs' key power in relation to nature conservation is the power to establish nature reserves. Paragraph 3 of Schedule 9 confers the power to establish nature reserves under section 21 of the 1949 Act on NPAs. This is probably the most important specific nature conservation power conferred on NPAs. By virtue of section 21(5) of the 1949 Act, all the powers relating to the establishment of nature reserves in Part 3 of the 1949 Act are conferred on NPAs. These include powers to compulsorily acquire land to establish nature reserves and to make byelaws for the protection of those reserves.

2.2 A nature reserve is defined in section 15 of the 1949 Act as ""nature reserve" means–

> *(a) land managed solely for a conservation purpose, or*
> *(b) land managed not only for a conservation purpose but also for a recreational purpose, if the management of the land for the recreational purpose does not compromise its management for the conservation purpose."*

2.3 A conservation purpose is defined in section 15(2) as the purpose of:

> *(a) providing, under suitable conditions and control, special opportunities for the study of,*
> *and research into, matters relating to the fauna and flora of Great Britain and the physical conditions in which they live, and for the study of geological and physiographical features of special interest in the area, or*
> *(b) preserving flora, fauna or geological or physiographical features of special interest in the area, or for both those purposes*

2.4 In order to exercise compulsory purchase powers to acquire land to establish a nature reserve, an NPA has to be satisfied that "*it is expedient in the national interest that it should be managed as a nature reserve*" and that it is unable, as respects any interest to be compulsorily acquired, to conclude on terms appearing to them reasonable a nature reserve agreement containing such provisions as in their opinion are required for securing that the land will be satisfactorily managed as a nature reserve: section 17 NPAC.

2.5 In practice, most nature reserves are established through nature reserve agreements with landowners under section 7 of the NERC Act 2006, section 16 of the Environment (Wales) Act 2016 or section 16 NPAC. Under section 7 NERC Act 2006 a management agreement can impose positive obligations on landowners in respect of the use of the land in question, provide for any matter for which a management scheme for a SSSI either provides or could provide, and provide for payments by either party to any other person, which can be enforced by the NPAs against successors in title to the original party to the agreement. The other management agreements referred to above have similar characteristics.

2.6 Under section 20 of the 1949 Act, NPAs can make byelaws for the protection of a nature reserve. The scope of matters that can be prohibited by such byelaws is very broad. They include prohibiting or restricting the entry into or movement within nature reserves of persons, vehicles, boats and animals, and killing, taking, or disturbing living creatures within the reserve. Section 20(2) states that byelaws made under section 20 shall not interfere with the exercise by any person of a right vested in that person as owner, lessee or occupier of land or with the exercise of any public right of way. Subsection 20(3) states that where the exercise of any right vested in a person is prevented or hindered by the coming into operation of byelaws under this section, that compensation is payable.

2.7 Any nature reserves established by a NPA may also be designated by Natural England or NRBW as national nature reserves under section 35 WCA 1981, where they consider that those reserves are of national importance. The effect of such designation would seem to be that Natural England and NRBW would assume the powers to make byelaws for such reserves.

## 3 SPECIFIC POWERS UNDER WCA 1981

### Management Agreements

3.1 Part II of the Wildlife and Countryside Act 1981 ("the WCA") confers various powers on NPAs, the most important being the power of a NPA under section 39 to enter into a management agreement for the purpose of conserving or enhancing the natural beauty or amenity of any land within the area or promoting its enjoyment by the public. Such agreements can impose restrictions on cultivation and the use of the land for agricultural purposes, and can confer power on NPAs to carry out works for the purpose of performing their functions under the 1949 Act and the 1968 Countryside Act.

### SSSIs, moors and heath

3.2 NPAs do not have power to notify areas of land as Sites of Special Scientific Interest ("SSSIs") under section 28 WCA 1981: such a power is reserved to Natural England and NRBW. However an NPA may if it is satisfied that it is expedient to do so by order (made by a statutory instrument) prevent moor or heath which has not been agricultural land for the last 20 years being converted into agricultural land, and prevent agricultural operations or any forestry operation which appears to the NPA to be likely to affect its character and appearance. Contravention of such an order is a criminal offence: section 42(5) WCA 1981. Under section 51, NPAs have powers of entry to ascertain whether an order should be made in relation to the land under section 42 or if an offence under that section is being, or has been, committed on the land in question.

## 4 BIODIVERSITY

4.1 In addition to the specific powers to establish and manage nature reserves within NPs, NPAs have an important role in managing and improving biodiversity in their capacity as LPAs. National planning policy already recognises that the environmental objective of sustainable development includes helping to improve biodiversity (paragraph 8(c) of the NPPF(2019)). In terms of plan-making, the NPPF expressly states that "plans should... identify and pursue opportunities for securing measurable net gains for biodiversity" (at paragraph 174(b). At the development management level, it states that "opportunities to incorporate biodiversity improvements in and around developments should be encouraged, especially where this can secure measurable net gains for biodiversity." (at paragraph 175(d)).

### Statutory duties in relation to biodiversity

4.2 In addition to those policy requirements in the NPPF (2019), NPAs are also under a general duty to conserve biodiversity pursuant to section 40 NERC Act 2006.

4.3 Section 40 NERC Act 2006 was limited to conserving biodiversity but did not impose a specific duty to consider enhancement or improvement of biodiversity. Improving and enhancing biodiversity is now likely to become an express obligation on NPAs should the provisions of Part 6 of the Environment Bill come into force. This Bill was introduced to Parliament in January 2020 and at the date of publication of this work had received its Second Reading in the House of Commons. The following is an outline of the provisions concerning biodiversity.[1]

---

1 Clause numbers refer to the clauses of the Bill as introduced to the House of Commons on 30 January 2020.

The new biodiversity gain objective

4.4 Clause 93 introduces a general duty on public authorities in England to conserve and enhance biodiversity (by amending section 40 NERC Act 2006). The proposed duty requires that "a public authority which has any functions exercisable in relation to England must from time to time consider what action the authority can properly take, consistently with the proper exercise of its functions, to further the general biodiversity objective". After that consideration, an authority must (unless it concludes that there is no new action it can properly take), determine "such policies and specific objectives as it considers appropriate for taking action to further the general biodiversity objective". The general biodiversity objective is described as "the conservation and enhancement of biodiversity in England through the exercise of functions in relation to England".

4.5 In the case of some NPAs, they may already have policies in their adopted plans which satisfy the biodiversity objective, in which case they are not under a duty to publish any additional or further plans. The South Downs National Park Authority, for example, has included a specific policy in its local plan referring to the need for development proposals to protect and provide more, better and joined up natural habitats.[2]

4.6 The Environment Bill also will require NPAs (in their capacities as LPAs) to publish biodiversity reports within three years (and thereafter every five years) which should include a summary of the action which the NPA has taken over the period covered by the report, and a summary of the authority's plans for complying with those duties over the next five years (see Clause 94). The report should also contain a summary of the action taken by the authority in relation to its new functions under the TCPA 1990

2 See Policy SD2 of the adopted SDNPA Local Plan and its reference to ecosystems services and accompanying technical advice notes https://www.southdowns.gov.uk/wp-content/uploads/2018/06/Chapter4-Core-Policies.pdf

in relation to the imposition of biodiversity gain requirements as conditions of planning permission (discussed further below).

Biodiversity gain as a condition of planning permission

4.7 Schedule 14 of the Bill makes provision for biodiversity gain to be a condition of planning permission in England, via a new Schedule 7A to be inserted into the TCPA 1990. This schedule makes provision for grants of planning permission to be subject to a condition to secure that the biodiversity gain objective is met.

4.8 The schedule contains detailed and relatively complex provisions specifying a methodology for calculating the biodiversity value attributable to development and its pre-development value. This is to be calculated by reference to the "biodiversity metric" which is document produced by the Secretary of State to measure in quantitative terms the biodiversity value or relative biodiversity value of a habitat.

4.9 In calculating the biodiversity value specifically attributable to development, registered off-site biodiversity gain (secured either by conservation covenants or planning obligations) can be taken into account via the recording of habitat enhancements in a biodiversity gain register maintained by the LPA. The biodiversity value of any "biodiversity credits" purchased for the development also forms part of the calculation of the biodiversity value attributable to development. The Bill envisages a 10% increase in value to be required by developments in order to meet the biodiversity gain objective, and value can only be taken into account if the LPA is satisfied it will be secured for at least 30 years.

4.10 Part 2 of Schedule 7A imposes a deemed planning condition on every grant of planning permission in the form of a pre-commencement condition requiring a biodiversity gain plan to be submitted to the LPA and approved which sets out not only the steps to be taken to minimise the adverse effect of the development on the biodiversity of onsite habitat and other habitat, but also the pre- and post-development value of the site calculated in accordance with the methodology described above.

### Local nature recovery strategies

4.11 Clause 96 of the Environment Bill will require English NPAs to prepare and publish a local nature recovery strategy for areas specified by the Secretary of State. The required content of such strategies is set out in Clause 97: the strategies are to include a description of the strategy area and its biodiversity, a local habitat map, a description of the opportunities for recovering or enhancing biodiversity, and the priorities, in terms of habitats and species, for recovering and enhancing biodiversity. They are also to include proposals as to potential measures relating to those priorities.

## 5 THE HABITATS REGULATIONS

5.1 In addition to the nature conservation and biodiversity provisions set out above, any NPA in its capacity as LPA when granting planning permission or adopting a local plan will be a competent authority and therefore subject to the obligations of the Conservation of Habitats and Species Regulations 2017 ("the Habitats Regulations")[3] which implement EU Council Directive 92/43/EEC on the Conservation of Natural Habitats of Wild Fauna and Flora ("the Habitats Directive"). The following is an outline of the main obligations of those Regulations and the Directive.[4]

---

3 SI No. 2017/1012

4 Upon the end of the transition period, the requirements of the 2017 Habitats Regulations will be retained subject to adjustments to reflect the UK's exit from the EU via the Conservation of Habitats and Species (Amendment) (EU Exit) Regulations 2019

## Appropriate assessments

5.2 For the purposes of an NPA's planning functions, the key provisions are Regulations 61, 63 – 64, and 68 which transpose Article 6(3) and 6(4) of the Directive.

5.3 Regulation 62 requires a competent authority (which would include an NPA) before deciding to undertake, or given any consent, permission or other authorisation for a plan or a project which is likely to have a significant effect on a European site and is not directly connected with or necessary to the management of that site, to make an "appropriate assessment" ("AA") of the plan or project for that site in view of that site's conservation objectives.

5.4 A European site is either a Special Area of Conservation ("a SAC") or a candidate SAC ("a cSAC"), a site (whether actually designated or proposed) of Community importance ("a SCI"), or a Special Protection Area ("SPA") classified under the EU Wild Birds Directive.[5] As of 31 October 2019, there are currently a total of 656 SACs in the United Kingdom. Of these, several are located in NPs and in some cases cover the majority of the NP.[6]

5.5 In terms of the contents of an AA, the English courts have stated that there is no specific format for an AA.[7] However, the standard such an AA must meet to comply with EU law was described by the CJEU in People over Wind & Sweetman v Coillte Teoranta (C-323/17) [2018] PTSR 1668 thus:

> *"[an AA] may not have lacunae and must contain complete, precise and definitive findings and conclusions*

---

5 Directive 2009/147/EC of the European Parliament and of the Council of 30 November 2009 on the conservation of wild birds

6 For example, the Dartmoor SAC covers most of the north and south of the National Park.

7 See the judgment of Lord Carnwath in R(Champion) v North Norfolk DC [2015] 1 WLR 3710

*capable of removing all reasonable scientific doubt as to the effects of the proposed works on the protected site concerned".*[8]

5.6 Pursuant to Regulation 63(6) in light of the conclusions of that assessment, an NPA as a competent authority may agree to a plan or project only after having ascertained that "it will not adversely affect the integrity of the European site". However, under Regulation 64 consent can be granted if the NPA is satisfied that "there being no alternative solutions, the project must be carried out for imperative reasons of overriding public interest" (the so-called "IROPI" test).

5.7 The regime under Article 6(3) and 6(4) is distinct from the broader duty on Member States which arises under Article 6(2) to "take appropriate steps to avoid" the significant deterioration of protected habitats or disturbance of protected species. Regulation 9(1) of the Habitats Regulations provides that public authorities when acting as competent authority or an appropriate authority "must exercise their functions which are relevant to nature conservation, including marine conservation, so as to secure compliance with the requirements of the Directives", meaning the Habitats Directive and the Birds Directive.

## Screening decisions

5.8 The Regulations require a two-stage process: an initial screening process in which the NPA must decide whether there is a risk of an adverse effect, followed by the appropriate assessment itself, which is a detailed assessment of the effect of development proposals of the site in light of the best scientific knowledge. A useful, practical summary of the two-stage approach and the

---

8 The so-called "precautionary principle" applied by the CJEU in this judgment was first enunciated by the CJEU in the Landelijke Vereniging tot Behoud van de Waddenzee v Staatssecretaris Van Landbouw, Natuurbeheer en Visserij (C127/02) [2005] 2 C.M.L.R. 31

thresholds for requiring an appropriate assessment is provided in the opinion of the Advocate General in People over Wind:

> *49. The threshold at the first stage of Article 6(3) is thus a very low one. It operates merely as a trigger, in order to determine whether an appropriate assessment must be undertaken of the implications of the plan or project for the conservation objectives of the site. The purpose of that assessment is that the plan or project in question should be considered thoroughly, on the basis of what the Court has termed 'the best scientific knowledge in the field'. Members of the general public may also be invited to give their opinion. Their views may often provide valuable practical insights based on their local knowledge of the site in question and other relevant background information that might otherwise be unavailable to those conducting the assessment.*
>
> *50. The test which that expert assessment must determine is whether the plan or project in question has 'an adverse effect on the integrity of the site', since that is the basis on which the competent national authorities must reach their decision. The threshold at this (the second) stage is noticeably higher than that laid down at the first stage. That is because the question (to use more simple terminology) is not 'should we bother to check?' (the question at the first stage) but rather 'what will happen to the site if this plan or project goes ahead; and is that consistent with "maintaining or restoring the favourable conservation status" of the habitat or species concerned?'. There is, in the present case, no dispute that if the road scheme is to proceed a part of the habitat will be permanently lost. The question is simply whether the scheme may be authorised without crossing that threshold and bringing into play the remaining elements of Article 6(3) (and, if necessary, Article 6(4)).*

## Mitigation measures

5.9 A recurrent issue in the application of the Habitats Regulations by local planning authorities has been whether or not mitigation measures proposed by the developer can be taken into account. Up until 2018, the view adopted by the English courts was that mitigation measures could be taken into account at the screening stage, in a line of authorities following the decision of Sullivan J in R (Hart District Council) v Secretary of State for Communities and Local Government [2008] 2 P & CR 16.[9] However, the CJEU in People Over Wind took a different view and held that taking into account at the screening stage measures intended to avoid or reduce the harmful effects of a plan or project would be liable to compromise the practical effect of the Habitats Directive. The outer boundaries of what is mitigation for these purposes is still being worked out: see R (Langton) v Secretary of State for Environment, Food and Rural Affairs [2018] EWHC 2190 (Admin)[10].

5.10 In terms of taking into account mitigation measures at the appropriate assessment stage itself, the CJEU has confirmed in a series of cases that an appropriate assessment cannot take into account the benefits of mitigation measures if those benefits are uncertain.[11]

---

9 See for example the judgments of Richards LJ in No Adastral New Town Ltd v Suffolk Coastal DC [2015] Env LR 28 at [72] – [74], Sales LJ in Smyth v SSCLG [2015] PTSR 1417 at [68] – [75]/

10 The case went on appeal but the Court of Appeal did not further consider this particular issue: [2019] 4 W.L.R. 151.

11 Cooperative Mobilisatoin For the Environment and Vereniging Leefmilieu Case C-293/17 and C-294/17 at [130] (the so-called "Dutch Nitrogen Cases") and Grace and Sweetman v An Board Pleanala Case C-164/17 [2019] PTSR 266.

# CHAPTER SIX

# WATER AND THE NATIONAL PARKS, THE BROADS AND AONBS

*James Neill and Nick Grant*

## 1. INTRODUCTION

1.1 The NPs have an important role to play in managing the water environment. In upland areas, schemes to re-wet moorland contribute to regulating the flow of water and reducing the likelihood and severity of floods. NPs are also a source of high-quality drinking water for millions of people. The lakes, rivers and Broads are rich in wildlife and provide excellent opportunities for recreation. However, they are also vulnerable to threats such as over-abstraction, flooding, drought, pollution and invasive species.

1.2 This chapter seeks to set out some of the key issues that development in the NPs and the Broads may give rise to in respect of rivers, watercourses and groundwater, and flooding. It starts by setting out the nature of property rights in respect of inland waters and waterways and the role of NPAs and the Broads Authority in making byelaws in respect of navigation, before taking a closer look at obligations on NPAs and the Broads Authority in respect of flood risk management, and impacts on watercourses and groundwater that development proposals may give rise. This chapter also touches on these issues in relation to AONBs albeit there are fewer specific statutory provisions of relevance in this context (and these are already referred to in Chapter 3).

## 2 NAVIGATION AND RIVERS

2.1 There are a number of private property rights associated with inland waters and waterways, including (for example) rights to the enjoyment and use of flowing water or a right to take or use water from a known channel.[1] Those are not the primary focus of this book and a detailed consideration of them is beyond its

---

1 See, for example *Halsbury's Laws* (Vol 100) (2018), para. 110 and following

scope. This section focuses on the rights of navigation and travel in rivers.[2]

## Ownership

2.2 A full review of matters of ownership of waterways is beyond the scope of this book. However, the following points are material for understanding rights of access to water. First, English law does not recognise the ownership of water. Instead, it recognises the ownership of "land covered by water": Moore v British Waterways Board [2013] Ch. 488, and the ownership of land next to water.

2.3 The Crown is, unless it has transferred the ownership, the owner of all land covered by the narrow seas adjoining the coast, or by arms of the sea or public navigable rivers, the foreshore, and the foreshore and bed of tidal rivers: see e.g. Lord Fitzhardinge v Purcell [1908] 2 Ch. 139, 146. The ownership of inland waters is different. By presumption of law, and in the absence of contrary evidence,[3] the ownership of the bed of a non-tidal river or stream belongs in equal halves to the owners of the riparian land either side: Moore [58]. Where the soil around a lake is owned by a proprietor, it is presumed the soil of the lake is owned by him (Mackenzie v Bankes (1878) 3 App Cas 1324, 1338). If a boundary passes along a pool it is taken to coincide with the centre line of the pool. If a lake is surrounded by multiple owners, the law is not settled.[4]

---

2 The regulation of reservoirs under the Reservoirs Act 1975 by the Environment Agency and National Resources Wales is also not considered in detail but may be relevant to the implementation of development proposals by a private reservoir owner.

3 It is perfectly possible for this presumption to be rebutted, as it is possible for an owner to retain one part of its property and part with another. Again the circumstances surrounding this are beyond the scope of this work, but see *Halsbury's Laws* Vol 100, para. 122 and following.

4 It has been both suggested and doubted in the House of Lords that any boundary lines would be drawn along to the middle of the lake – compare Mackenzie v Bankes (1878) 3 App. Cas. 1324, 13338 with Bristow v Cormican (1878) 3 App

2.4 Given the importance of discerning who is a local authority for determining who exercises planning functions, it should be also noted that where a parish comes down as far as a riverbank, there is a prima facie assumption that the parish extends to the middle of the river, and where two parishes are separated by a river, the centre of the river is the presumptive line between them: R v The Inhabitants of Landulph (1834) 1 Mood & Rob. 393, 174 E.R. 135. The same applies to counties, save where a statute otherwise provides: R v The Inhabitants of the County of Brecon (1849) 15 Q.B.R. 813, 117 E.R. 665, 670.

## Riparian Rights

2.5 A riparian owner is one whose land is in actual daily contact with the water, (whether laterally or vertically), whether that water is tidal or non-tidal river, a lake, or the sea: Lyon v Fishmongers' Company (1876) 1 App. Cas. 662. Where the land abuts a tidal river or the sea, this is so even if the foreshore is left bare at low tide: Lyon v Fishmonger's Company at p. 683. If in the course of time the river recedes from the land owing to natural silting up or artificial reclamation, the riparian owner may exercise his right of access over the accreted or reclaimed land: Attorney-General of Southern Nigeria v John Holt & Co (Liverpool) Ltd [1915] AC 599, 621 (PC).

2.6 Broadly, riparian owners[5] have two broad sets of rights – rights of access, and rights to the continued natural flow of the watercourse. This is so whether or not they own the bed of the river: Moore [66]. This book focuses on rights of access,[6] which are

a) access to and egress from the water: Lyon v Fishmongers' Company;

Cas 641, 666.

5 And his lessee or licensee unless the lease or license express otherwise: Marshall p. 172-173.

6 For detailed commentary on the rights to continued natural flow of watercourses, see *Halsbury's Laws of England* Vol 100 (2018) para. 133 and following.

b) to pass or repass over the shore or bed at all states of the water for that purpose: Attorney-General of Southern Nigeria v John Holt & Co (Liverpool) Ltd; and

c) A "reasonable right of stopping" for such period as is necessary to load or unload, and (if the waters are tidal and the vessels cannot be unloaded in one tide) to keep them there until the operation is completed. This cannot be used to impede the rights of other riparian owners or the public rights of navigation, and (unless the riparian owner also owns the bed of the water) does not extend to a permanent right to moor vessels: Moore [63]-[66].

2.7 Such rights do not extend to having any particular depth of water maintained: Tate and Lyle Industries Ltd v Greater London Council [1983] 2 AC 509, 532. A riparian owner who does not own the bed cannot put down a pier, or anything which disturbs the foreshore or other land which he does not own: Marshall v The Ulleswater Steam Navigation Co (1871) L.R. 7 Q.B. 166, 172-173. One who does, can: Moore [58].

2.8 Such riparian rights of access are wholly separate from the public right of navigation. Where a river is navigable, the interaction of the two was explained as follows by the Lord Chancellor in Lyon v Fishmongers' Company p 673:

> *"A riparian owner on a navigable river has, of course, superadded to his riparian rights, the right of navigation over every part of the river, and on the other hand his riparian rights must be controlled in this respect, that whereas, in a non-navigable river, all the riparian owners might combine to divert, pollute, or diminish the stream, in a navigable river the public right of navigation would intervene, and would prevent this being done."*

2.9 So, for example, the riparian owners on a navigable river may moor a floating wharf or erect a jetty (subject to issues of trespass above) provided they do not actually interfere with the right of navigation (see e.g. A-G v Terry (1874) 9 Ch App 423).

## Rights of Navigation

2.10 As the soil of tidal water is prima facie vested in the crown, there is a general public right of navigation in tidal waters: Denaby and Cadeby Main Collieries Ltd v Anson [1911] 1 K.B. 171, 198. The right is paramount, so any disposition of tidal waters by the crown is subject to that public right: Fitzhardinge v Purcell, p. 167.

2.11 In non-tidal waters there is no such presumption. A public right of navigation can be established by immemorial usage (see Orr Ewing v Colquhoun (1887) 2 App. Cas. 839), Act of Parliament (or order made thereunder) (as in R v Betts (1850) 16 QB 1022), or by express grant by the owner of the soil of the river.

2.12 In the Broads, section 8(5) of the NSBA 1988, provides that

> *(5) Subject to any provisions made by or under this Act, the navigation area shall be open to any person (upon payment by him of all navigation charges) for—*
>
> *(a) navigation;*
>
> *(b) the shipping and unshipping of goods; and*
>
> *(c) the embarking and landing of passengers.*

2.13 Section 74 of the 1949 Act provides that the provisions of Part V of the 1949 Act (access to open country) apply equally to waterways in NPs.[7]

[7] See Chapter 8 for more detail on other access rights

2.14 The essence of the public right of navigation in tidal waters was described by Lord Diplock in Tate & Lyle at p. 545 as:

> *"A public right of navigation in navigable waters that form part of a port is a right enjoyed by every member of the public to pass and repass over the whole of the surface of the water in vessels of such draught as the depth of water below any particular part of the surface permits and to keep such vessels stationary in the water for a reasonable time for navigational purposes in the course of a voyage (eg waiting for a tide) or for the purpose of loading, unloading or transhipping goods or passengers or waiting to do so."*

2.15 Such rights must be exercised reasonably. It does not include the permanent right to occupy any stretch of water: Moore [60]-[61]. Nor does it generally include the right to land persons or goods on the foreshore or banks, save where there is permission, usage, or necessity (Behrens v Richards [1905] 2 Ch 614) or the right of towing along the bank save where that right otherwise exists (Ball v Herbert (1789) 3 Term Rep 253).

2.16 In non-tidal waters, the right is similar, but more restricted: it is confined to the extent of the user or grant acquired (see e.g. Orr Ewing v Colquhoun), is subservient to the rights of the landowners and their assignees unless otherwise provided by the Act of Parliament of deed of grant (Original Hartlepool Collieries Co v Gibb (1877) 5 ChD 713), and does not carry a right of fishing or fowling (Orr Ewing v Colquhoun).

2.17 Once such rights are established, they may not be obstructed by any party without statutory authority (Orr Ewing). However, where obstructions which existed prior to the right of navigation being established may not be removed, as the right was acquired subject to that obstruction (Orr Ewing). The Secretary of State may, under the Transport and Works Act 1992, make a works order relating to the construction or operation of an inland waterway, or the carrying out of works that interfere with rights of navigation in waters within or adjacent to England and Wales.

2.18 At common law the owner of a bed of a navigable river is not obliged to clear the channel of natural obstructions, nor is a navigation authority save for the purposes of navigation (Cracknell v Thetford Corpn (1869) LR 4 CP 629). A navigation authority must, however take reasonable care that the public can navigate without danger to life or property.

### Management and supervision of inland waterways

2.19 The Crown under royal prerogative exercised from the earliest times a jurisdiction over ports, harbours, rivers, creeks, arms of the sea and their navigation. This has now devolved to a large number of navigation authorities whose rights and functions depend on the particular statutes governing them. The largest navigation authorities are the Canal and River Trust ("CRT"), the Broads Authority, and the Environment Agency ("EA"). A list of UK navigation authorities is available on the website of British Marine.[8] The position as to who is a navigation authority is not static, as both the CRT and the EA may apply to the Secretary of State for an order transferring the functions of a navigation authority to it (British Waterways Act 1983 section 10 and Water Resources Act 1991 Sch. 2).

#### The Broads

2.20 The duties of the Broads Authority have already been outlined in Chapter 1. Part II of the NSBA 1988 concerns the Navigation Area. The Navigation Area is, per s. 8(1)

> *subject to any variation for the time being in force by virtue of an order under subsection (3) below—*

---

8 https://britishmarine.co.uk/Services/Business-Support/Technical-Support/Guidance-and-Advice/Commercial-Vessels/Navigation-Authorities-UK

> *(a) those stretches of the rivers Bure, Yare and Waveney, and their tributaries, branches and embayments (including Oulton Broad) which, at the passing of this Act, were in use for navigation by virtue of any public right of navigation;*
>
> *(b) the banks of the waterways which make up those stretches; and*
>
> *(c) Haddiscoe New Cut and its banks; [and*
>
> *(d) Breydon Water and the Lower Bure]*
>
> *but does not include any part of the Haven or any part of any bank which lies above the level of mean high water spring tides (in the case of a tidal waterway) or above the mean water level (in any other case).*

2.21 The Broads Authority's functions are outlined in section 10 and Schedule 5 of the NSBA 1988, and the Broads Authority Act 2009. It must both maintain the navigation area for the purposes of navigation to such standard is appears to it to be reasonable required, and take such steps to improve and develop the navigation areas as it thinks fit (section 10(1)).

2.22 To further this function, the Broads Authority is given wide ranging powers. These include:

a) The power to provide facilities, construct, alter or renew works, carry out dredging, and undertake other such activities. It may carry out works and do other things in relation to any adjacent waters in, or over which, it has sufficient rights or interests for the improvement of navigation of those waters (section 10(2A)).

b) Make byelaws for the good management of the navigation area, the conservation of its natural beauty and amenities, and the promotion of its use for purposes of recreation (section 10(3)). These can include byelaws made for the purposes of, for example, regulating the use of waterways, prescribing navigational rules, requiring those in charge of boats to carry certain qualifications, and requiring the registration of craft (see paras. 4-5 of Sched 5). It may also make byelaws for the purpose of providing for the registration of vessels in the navigation or adjacent waters, for the determination and recovery of tolls (see section 11 Broads Authority Act 2009).

c) It must appoint a navigation officer and may appoint any deputies, who will be wardens for byelaws purposes and may give directions for, for example, regulating the time and manner of vessels arrivals, regulating the position of vessels in the navigation area, or prohibiting the mooring of vessels (section 10(6),(7),(13), Part II Schedule 5).

d) Give general directions in respect of vessels in, or proposing to enter, or leaving the navigation area, for the purpose of promoting conditions conducive to the ease, convenience or safety of navigation and the safety of persons and property in the navigation area (Broads authority Act 2009 section 4(1)). This can include designating routes for navigation, securing that vessels only move at certain times, limiting speed, or prohibiting entry into the navigation area by vessels at times of poor visibility. These can apply to all vessels or designated classes, the whole navigation area or designated parts, at all times or at designated times. (see generally section 4). The Navigation Officer may also give special directions to particular vessels (see section 6). The master of a vessel who fails to comply with a general or special direction is guilty of offence and liable to a fine (Section 7).

e) Designate any part of the navigation area for the loading or unloading of relevant goods, and provide that such goods thereafter cannot be deposited or received elsewhere (Section 10).

f) Require the removal of unsafe vessels (or remove them itself) (section 19-20).

g) Designate zones and times in which waterskiing and wakeboarding are permitting in the navigation area, issue permits for the carrying out of such activities, and display signs and give directions to persons intending to carry out such activities (sections 26-29 Broads Authority Act 2009).

h) Lop or cut any part of a hedge tree or shrub projecting into over or beneath the waters of the navigation area or is diseased and is likely to case danger by falling into the navigation area (section 39 Broads Authority Act 2009).

2.23 The NSBA 1988 also prohibits any person from altering, renewal constructing or extending works, save in very limited circumstances, without a license from the Broads Authority. Undertaking works without a license is an offence punishable by a fine not exceeding level 3 on the standard scale (£1,000 at the time of writing) (See sections 11-12).

Other authorities

2.24 Outside of the Broads, as noted above, which authority constitutes the navigation authority is something of a moveable feast. The only NPAs featured on the British Marine website are the Like District NPA and the Lock Lomond and the Trossachs NPA.

2.25 In areas designated as NPs, s. 13 of the 1949 Act permits LPAs to carry out such work and do such other things as may appear to them necessary or expedient for facilitating the use of the waterway by the public for sailing, boating, boating or fishing. Section 75 of the 1949 Act allows an access order specified under section 74 to specify works to be carried out under section 13.

2.26 LPAs are also given the power to make byelaws for waterways to which the public are given access under an access agreement or order. These may, for example, prohibit or restrict the use of the waterway, either generally or as specified. See section 90(1) and (3) of the 1949 Act. These byelaws may be enforced by County or District councils (section 90(6) of the 1949 Act). The Secretary of State or the NRBW may require councils to make such bylaws and, if they do not may themselves make the bylaws (section 91 of the 1949 Act). Section 106 of the 1949 Act contains supplementary provisions, including the power to enforce the byelaws made. Section 106A contains supplementary provisions for byelaws made by the NRBW. A local authority may appoint such wardens as are necessary or expedient (section 92 of the 1949 Act).

2.27 LPAs whose area includes any part of a NP may also make byelaws for the prohibition or restriction of traffic of any description on any lake in the park: section 13(1) Countryside Act 1968. A "lake" here includes any expanse of water other than a river or canal (section 13(13)), but these provisions do not apply to any lake owned or managed by any statutory undertakers (section 13(7)).[9] Byelaws may, for example, prescribe rules of navigation, impose speed limits, or require the use of silencers (section 13(3)). Section 13(2) provides that the power may be exercised for ensuring the safety of persons on the like, regulating all forms of sport or recreation involving the use of boats or vessels, conserving the amenity and natural beauty of the lake and surrounding area, or preventing nuisance or damage. Such byelaws cannot be made to extinguish any public right of way over any waters, but shall apply (unless expressly provided otherwise) to all persons exercising any such public right of way (section 13(5)). Section 106 of the 1949 Act is also applied to byelaws made under this section (section 13(8)), save for in Wales where it is the Local Government Byelaws (Wales) Act 2012 that

---

9 A "statutory undertaker" has the meaning assigned in s. 262 TCPA 1990 – s. 49(1) Countryside Act 1968.

applies (see section 13(8A)). Sections 92(1),(2) and (4) of the 1949 Act also apply (section 13(10)).

2.28 Where the waterways fall outside an NP (e.g., an AONB), the role and powers of the navigation authority will depend on the enabling statute.

2.29 The Canal and River Trust is under a duty to maintain both commercial waterways and waterways principally available for cruising, fishing and other recreational activities ("cruising waterways") (section 105 Transport Act 1968). This duty is enforceable by the High Court (section 106A Transport Act 1968). In formulating any proposals, it must pay regard to a number of statutory considering which include furthering the conservation and enhancement of natural beauty, the desirability of preserving public freedom of access to places of natural beauty, and protecting cruising waterways for future use (section. 22 British Waterways Act 1995). It may also make byelaws for the use of its canals, alongside a number of other miscellaneous powers.[10]

2.30 The Environment Agency and NRBW have functions as navigation authority, harbour authority or conservancy authority in relation to some inland waterways in England and Wales. They may, where necessary or expedient for the purposes of their statutory functions make byelaws prohibiting inland waters from being used for boating, or regulating the way in which waters may be uses for those purposes – though such byelaws cannot apply to any tidal or "discrete waters" (i.e. lakes or groups that do not discharge into other inland waters) or inland waters which have a different navigation authority. They may also make byelaws for inland waters over which there is a public right of navigation, and is not under the control of a navigation authority or the navigation authority is prescribed by the Secretary of State as being unable to carry out its functions (paras. 1-2 of Sched. 25 Water Resources Act 1991). They are also given the power to apply to

[10] *Halsbury's Laws*, Vol 100 para. 199-200.

the Secretary of State or Welsh Ministers to levy tolls on navigable waters which are not subject to the control of another navigation authority, harbour authority, or conservancy authority (section 143(1) Water Resources Act 1991). Furthermore, section 6 Environment Act 1995 imposes a duty on them to promote the conservation and enhancement of the natural beauty and amenity of inland and coastal waters and land associated with those, the conservation of flora and fauna dependent on the aquatic environment, and the use of such waters and land for recreational purposes.

2.31 Every relevant undertaker under the Water Industry Act 1991 (i.e. companies appointed by the Secretary of State) may also make byelaws (section 157(1) Water Industry Act 1991).

## 3 FLOODING

3.1 This section sets out the statutory and policy framework for the management of flood risk in England and Wales. As is explained in further detail below, whilst NPAs do not have specific statutory duties in relation to the management of flood risk, in their capacities as local planning authorities they have an important role to play in managing flood risk.

### The Flood and Water Management Act 2010

3.2 In England and Wales, the key statute specifying various duties in relation to flood management is the Flood and Water Management Act 2010 ("FWMA 2010"). This sets out which authorities are responsible for managing flood risk.

3.3 Under the Act, the Environment Agency has the strategic role in relation to all flooding, whether from rivers, sea water, surface runoff and groundwater, as well as coastal erosion and flood risk from reservoirs in England. Pursuant to section 7 of it is under a duty to produce a flood and coastal erosion risk management strategy in England ("FCERM"). The Welsh Ministers are under a duty to produce a similar strategy in relation to Wales.

3.4 The Act also imposes various duties on Lead Local Flood Authorities ("LLFAs") and Risk Management Authorities ("RMAs"), including a duty to co-operate with each and act in a manner that is consistent with the FCERM.

3.5 Under the Act, LLFAs' duties include a duty to develop, apply, maintain and monitor strategies for local flood risk management in their areas, and to prepare and maintain a preliminary flood risk assessment, flood hazard maps, flood risk maps and flood risk management plans.

3.6 NPAs are not designated as LLFAs, which are defined (in England) as the unitary authority for the area, or if there is no unitary authority, the county council (see section 6 FWMA). In Wales, the LLFAs are county councils or the county borough council for the area.

3.7 Nor are they designated as RMAs, which are defined as the Environment Agency, NRBW, LLFAs, district councils, internal drainage boards, water companies and highway authorities.

## Flood risk and NPA's planning functions

3.8 The main responsibilities of NPAs in relation to flood risk derive from their local plan preparation and development management functions as LPAs. Set out below is an overview of the main policies which apply to NPAs in relation to flood risk.

3.9 In their capacity as local planning authorities, NPAs when preparing their local plans must undertake a Strategic Flood Risk Assessment to fully understand the flood risk in the area to inform their local plan preparation (see NPPF (2019) paragraph 155). They have to apply a sequential approach risk-based approach to the location of development. The aim of the sequential test (as described in the NPPF (2019) at paragraph 158) is to:

> *"steer new development to areas with the lowest risk of flooding. Development should not be allocated or permitted if there are reasonably available sites appropriate for the proposed development in areas with a lower risk of flooding. The strategic flood risk assessment will provide the basis for applying this test. The sequential approach should be used in areas known to be at risk now or in the future from any form of flooding."*

3.10 If it is not possible for development to be located in zones with a lower risk of flooding, the NPPF (2019) states that the exception test may be applied (paragraph 159). For the exception test to be passed it should be demonstrated that:

> *"(a) the development would provide wider sustainability benefits to the community that outweigh the flood risk; and*
>
> *(b) the development will be safe for its lifetime taking account of the vulnerability of its users, without increasing flood risk elsewhere, and, where possible, will reduce flood risk overall"*

3.11 Paragraphs 163 – 165 of the NPPF (2019) set out how flood risk should be taking into account when determining planning applications. Paragraph 163 states that development should only be allowed in areas at risk of flooding where, in light of a site-specific flood-risk assessment, it can be demonstrated that:

> *a) within the site, the most vulnerable development is located in areas of lowest*
> *flood risk, unless there are overriding reasons to prefer a different location;*

> *b) the development is appropriately flood resistant and resilient;*
> *c) it incorporates sustainable drainage systems, unless there is clear evidence that*
> *this would be inappropriate;*
> *d) any residual risk can be safely managed; and*
> *e) safe access and escape routes are included where appropriate, as part of an agreed emergency plan.*

## 4 WATER QUALITY

4.1 Improving water quality to watercourses falls within the key conservation purposes of NPAs. The Broads Authority for instance has as one of its central aims the restoration of clear water and life to the lakes and rivers of the Broads.

4.2 However, as with flooding, NPAs do not have any specific, additional duties in relation to preserving or protecting water quality over and above the duties that arise by virtue of their roles as LPAs. The Environment Agency therefore continues to play its key role in regulating any contamination of watercourses within NPs and if necessary bringing any enforcement action under the EA 1995.

4.3 However, the most significant way in which issues regarding water supply and quality are likely to arise for NPAs is as material considerations when NPAs determine planning applications.

### Water quality and planning

4.4 National PPG states that water quality is "only likely to be a significant planning concern" where a proposal would:

> *Water quality is only likely to be a significant planning concern when a proposal would:*

*involve physical modifications to a water body such as flood storage areas, channel diversions and dredging, removing natural barriers, construction of new locks, new culverts, major bridges, new barrages/dams, new weirs (including for hydropower) and removal of existing weirs; and/or indirectly affect water bodies, for example,*

- *as a result of new development such as the redevelopment of land that may be affected by contamination, mineral workings, water or wastewater treatment, waste management facilities and transport schemes including culverts and bridges;*
- *result in runoff into surface water sewers that drain directly, or via combined sewers, into sensitive waterbodies e.g. water bodies with local, national or international habitat designations;*
- *through a lack of adequate infrastructure to deal with wastewater*
- *through a lack of adequate infrastructure to deal with wastewater where development occurs in an area where there is a strategic water quality plan e.g. Nutrient Management Plans, River Basin Management Plans, water cycle studies, diffuse water pollution plans or sewerage undertakers' drainage strategies which set out strategies to manage water quality locally and help deliver new development.*[11]

## The Water Framework Directive

4.5 Any impacts on water quality will need to be addressed in an Environmental Impact Assessment ("EIA") accompanying a

[11] PPG Paragraph 16 Reference ID: 34-016-20140306

planning application which should assess any significant likely effects on water quality of a watercourse. However, in addition to the general requirement under the EIA Regs (and – if a European protected site or species is likely to be adversely affected – the Habitats Regulations[12]), the Water Framework Directive[13] is also relevant ("the WFD").

4.6 A discussion of the detailed scope and obligations of the WFD is beyond the scope of this chapter. However, in summary the purpose of the WFD (which was adopted and came into force in 2000) is to establish a framework for the protection of inland surface waters, estuaries, coastal waters and groundwater. The framework for delivering the Directive in the UK is through River Basin Management Planning. The WFD places a responsibility on Member States to try and ensure that all inland and coastal waters reach at least "good status" (or good ecological potential for artificial or heavily modified water bodies). The Directive uses five status classifications for normal waterbodies: High, Good, Moderate, Poor and Bad and allows for extended deadlines or less stringent objectives to be set for water bodies, should certain conditions be met.

4.7 To achieve the target of reaching good status or above, Member States are required to implement management planning at river basin level, linking with other key policy areas such as agriculture, land use, biodiversity, tourism, recreation and flood protection. This is done through the publication of river basin management plans (RBMPs) by the Environment Agency which set out a programme of measures to be implemented over six-year cycles aimed at improving the status of waterbodies[14]. Such RBMPs are

12 Discussed further in Chapter 5 above

13 The Water Framework Directive (2000/60/EC) as amended by Directives 2008/105/EC, 2013/39/EU and 2014/101/EU.

14 The Environment Agency is due to publish its next River Basin Management Plan in 2021

established in consultation with River Basin District Liaison Panels (RBLPs) which should include NPAs.

4.8 The WFD is implemented in England and Wales by the Water Environment (Water Framework Directive) (England and Wales) Regulations 2017 ("the WER Regs").[15] There is a general duty on all public bodies including NPAs to provide information and such assistance as the Environment Agency may reasonably seek in connection with exercising their responsibilities for implementing the WFD. Where this has been requested by the Environment Agency, an NPA should notify the Environment Agency if planning permission is granted for a new development likely to lead to deterioration of a water body.

4.9 Furthermore, any public body (which would include NPAs) must, in exercising their functions so far as affecting a river basin district,[16] have regard to the river basin management plan for that district as approved by the appropriate authority i.e for England, the Environment Agency and in Wales, National Resources for Wales (Regulation 33 of the WER Regs).

4.10 The WFD is also a relevant consideration as a result of national policy. The PPG states that:

> *"In the few cases where a detailed assessment indicates that development will have a significant adverse impact on water quality then the proposed development will only be acceptable where the conditions in Article 4.7 of the Water Framework Directive having regard to the river basin management plan. The Environment Agency may be able to advise on meeting those requirements."*

---

15 SI 2017/407

16 Whilst "relevant functions" under the WER Regs do not include functions of LPAs under the Planning Acts, Regulation 33 applies to any function at all and so would include the planning functions of an NPA.

4.11 Article 4.7 of the WFD states that Member States will not be in breach of the WDD when:

> *Member States will not be in breach of this Directive when:*
> *— failure to achieve good groundwater status, good ecological status*
> *or, where relevant, good ecological potential or to prevent deterioration in the status of a body of surface water or groundwater is the result of new modifications to the physical characteristics of a surface water body or alterations to the level of bodies of groundwater, or*
> *— failure to prevent deterioration from high status to good status of a body of surface water is the result of new sustainable human development activities and all the following conditions are met:*
> *(a) all practicable steps are taken to mitigate the adverse impact on the status of the body of water;*
> *(b) the reasons for those modifications or alterations are specifically set out and explained in the river basin management plan required under Article 13 and the objectives are reviewed every six years;*
> *(c) the reasons for those modifications or alterations are of overriding public interest and/or the benefits to the environment and to society of achieving the objectives set out in paragraph 1 are outweighed by the benefits of the new modifications or alterations to human health, to the maintenance of human safety or to sustainable development, and*
> *(d) the beneficial objectives served by those modifications or alterations of the water body cannot for reasons of technical feasibility or disproportionate cost be achieved by other means, which are a significantly better environmental option*

## 5 WATER ABSTRACTION

5.1 NPs often contain important aquifers providing water for public consumption. The South Downs National Park for example has one of the largest aquifers in the UK, due to its unique geology and the permeability of its chalk. A detailed discussion of the regime for water abstraction in England and Wales however is beyond the scope of this work. Water abstraction i.e. taking water from a surface source or from an underground source is regulated under the Water Resources Act 1991 (as amended by the Water Act 2003 and Water Act 2014) by either the Environment Agency or NRBW. However, impacts on those aquifers as a result of development will be relevant when determining a planning application.

# CHAPTER SEVEN

# PUBLIC RIGHTS OF WAY

*Stephen Morgan*

## 1 INTRODUCTION

1.1 Public rights of way are minor public highways that exist for the benefit of the community at large, in much the same way as the public road network does. They are the most widely recognised facility that gives the public the opportunity to enjoy the countryside. Public rights of way may be exercised on foot, bicycle, horse or in a motorised vehicle. These rights should be distinguished from other rights such as rights to roam and village green rights. The former are covered in the next chapter, whilst the latter are outside the scope of this book.

1.2 The exercising of these rights allows for people to access and recreate in the countryside. Walking is reported and understandably the most popular activity in all the national parks; cycling is of course also very popular. Both are also popular in the AONBs as well as the Broads. For both walking and cycling, there are recommended trails. In terms of walking and horse riding, footpaths and bridleways are key, but of course these can be accessed and used together with public roads and pavements.

1.3 The legal nature and extent of these rights is outlined below but use of the countryside should also be in accordance with Countryside Code which applies to all parts of the countryside in England and Wales and aims to help everyone respect, protect and enjoy the outdoors in terms of respecting other people, protecting the natural environment and enjoying the outdoors.[1]

1.4 Footpaths and bridleways do not usually have the same obvious physical presence as carriageway highways. They are not usually made up and are narrower than carriageway highways. They may not even have any obvious markings, save for perhaps wear and tear. However, footpaths and bridleways have gained increasing significance over the last century by providing access into the

---

1 See Natural England's The Countryside Code – online version at: https://www.gov.uk/government/publications/the-countryside.

countryside for the increasing number who wish to recreate there, including ramblers and leisure horse riders.

1.5 Reflecting that significance, there has been pressure to recognise and thus help to protect such public rights of way where necessary through legislation, as the common law and existing legislation was not adequately doing so. The mapping exercise to enable this was provided for in the National Parks and Access to the Countryside Act 1949 ("the NPAC 1949") and modified by later legislation, in particular the Wildlife and Countryside Act 1981 ("WCA 1981"). The process for confirming such rights is addressed in the section 4 of this Chapter.

1.6 There was also pressure for a more general right to roam, and the Countryside and Rights of Way Act 2000 ("CROW 2000") has now established a more general right of access to some open areas across the countryside which, as indicated above, is addressed in the next Chapter. However, there is no right to wander at common law and the statutory right to roam applies to open access land including mountains, moors, heaths, downs, common land and some land around the England Coast Path.

1.7 This Chapter covers the legal nature of public rights of way; how they are created and recorded and how that record is updated to reflect new evidence and relevant events; who is responsible for their maintenance and repair; provisions for dealing with interference with these rights; and the removal and diversion of public rights of way. This is set out in the following sections:

(2) Nature and Extent of Public Rights of Way
(3) Creation of Public Rights of Way
(4) Recording of Public Rights of Way and Modification Orders
(5) Maintenance and Protection of Public Rights of Way
(6) Diversions and Extinguishments

1.8 This Chapter provides only a brief outline of what is a detailed and complex legislative framework. Any reader who requires a more detailed analysis of any of the aspects or issues may wish to refer to the several excellent texts and in particular *Highway Law* by Stephen Sauvain QC (fifth edition, with the sixth edition due to be published late 2020) and *Public Rights of Way: The Essential Law* by Angela Sydenham (2019), both of which works are referenced in this Chapter.

## 2 NATURE AND EXTENT OF PUBLIC RIGHTS OF WAY

### Characteristics of a public right of way

2.1 The terms 'highway' and 'public rights of way' are often used interchangeably, although the former is sometimes used to denote the physical route rather than the right itself[2]. A highway is essentially a public right to pass over a defined linear route and consists of the following elements[3]:

(a) The way must be open to the public at large;
(b) The public must have a right to use the way;
(c) The public right must be primarily for passage; and
(d) The public right of way must follow a defined route.

2.2 Public rights of way have to be distinguished from other rights. For example a private right of way is an easement (i.e. a right over land for the benefit of other land) and cannot be used by the public generally. Nonetheless, a public footpath or bridleway may also carry private rights. These rights may be vested in a third party as an easement or reserved to the landowner.

---

2 Angela Sydenham's *Public Rights of Way ad Access to Land* (4th Edition) at 1.1 on p.1.

3 This is dealt with in detail in Chapter 1 of Stephen Sauvain QC's *Highway Law* (5th Edition); and see also Chapter 2 of Angela Sydenham's Public Rights of Way and Access to Land (2019).

2.3 As addressed in section 4 of this Chapter, the starting point for ascertaining the location and category of any public rights of way in any given area is the definitive map and statement, which is a record maintained by the surveying authority of the such rights within its area[4]. The councils which are the highway authorities are also the surveying authorities. These are the councils of the county, metropolitan district or London borough. In Wales, the county or county borough is the surveying authority[5].

2.4 If there is no formally recognised public right of way, or right to roam, the public may still be able to access private land if, as pointed out on the Government website[6]:

(a) The land, although not shown on the definitive map and statement, was used as a public right of way in the past as might be indicated by old maps and documents.

(b) The land was accessed by the public for at least 20 years and nobody had asked them to stop.

(c) The landowner has given permission ('permissive access').

## Categories of public rights of way

2.5 The public rights of way, which are shown on a definitive map and may be waymarked in different colours, are made up of:

(a) **Footpaths** (waymark colour yellow[7]): over which the right of way is on foot only[8]. There may be issues over what the walker can lawfully take with him or her on a footpath. Bicycles are not considered to be a natural accompaniment of a walker and pushing a bicycle on a

---

4 S.53 of the WCA 1981.

5 HA 1980, s.31(7).

6 https://www.gov.uk/right-of-way-open-access-land.

7 Waymarking public rights of way, Natural England.

8 WCA 1981, s.66(1).

footpath would be a trespass. Dogs are however regarded as a usual accompaniment, although there does not appear to be any definitive legal judgment to that effect. Also, there are several offences that relate to dogs, particularly under the Dog (Protection of Livestock) Act 1953. For example, where there are sheep on enclosed land a dog must be kept on a lead or under close control. In the nineteenth century case of R v Mathias (1861) 2 F & F 570, 175 ER 1191 the jury decided that a perambulator was a usual accompaniment. It was said in that case:

> "*...such things as are usual accompaniment of a large class of foot passengers, being so small and light, as neither to be a nuisance to other passengers nor injurious to the soil.*"

Use of a footpath by horse riders or cyclists is not itself a criminal offence (subject to any local orders and bylaws), although it is a trespass against the landowner. Bridleway rights may be acquired over a footpath by long use and such long use could change a footpath into a restricted byway (see below)[9]. There is no right to ride a bicycle over a footpath. However, as for horse riders, a sufficient number of people riding bicycles on a public footpath could amount to a deemed dedication of a restricted byway[10]. It should also be noted that the Cycle Tracks Act 1984 enables footpaths to be converted into cycle tracks. These statutory creations are not shown on the definitive map and confer a right of way for pedal cycles, and usually a right on foot.

(b) **Bridleways** (waymark colour blue): these can be used by pedestrians, horse riders and cyclists, although the latter

[9] With regard to the maintenance consequences see HA 1980, s.31(10A) as inserted by the NERC Act 2006, s.68(3).

[10] NERC Act 2006, s.68.

must give way to people on foot or on horseback[11]. Horse is defined to include pony, ass or mule, but not llama. A bicycle does not include a mechanically propelled vehicle intended or adapted for use on the roads, although an electrically assisted pedal cycle is not a mechanically propelled vehicle[12]. However, cycle riding might be forbidden by local orders or bylaws[13]. Whether or not driftway rights (a right to drive cattle or sheep) exist will depend upon the evidence.[14]

(c) **Restricted byways** (waymark colour plum): these are carriageways over which the right of way is for all types of traffic save for mechanically propelled vehicles (which does not include an electrically assisted pedal cycle[15]). Most of these are former Roads Used as Public Paths ('RUPPs') which were re-designated *en masse* by the CROW 2000 from 2 May 2006. However, the effect of s. 67 of the Natural Environment and Rural Communities Act 2006 ('NERC Act 2006') is that rights for mechanically propelled vehicles are extinguished unless one of the exceptions applies. The result is that the RUPP would thus be reclassified as a restricted byway. As a result, new public rights of way for mechanically propelled vehicles will only be created if they are expressly granted or they apply to a road intended to be used for mechanically propelled vehicles.

(d) **Byways open to all traffic (BOATs)** (waymark colour red): these are carriageways over which the right of way is on foot, on horseback and for all vehicular traffic (including mechanically propelled vehicles) but which

---

11 CA 1968, s.30.

12 Road Traffic Act 1988, s.189(1)(c) and HA 1980, s.31(12)).

13 CA 1968, s.30(2) and Local Government Act 1972, s.235.

14 WCA 1981, s.66(1); and HA 1980, s.329(1).

15 S.31(12) into the HA 1980 inserted by NERC Act 2006, s.68(4).

are used mainly for the purposes for which footpaths ad bridleways are used (i.e. by walkers and horse riders) [16].

2.6 Section 34 of the Road Traffic Act 1988 makes it unlawful for a person to drive a mechanically propelled vehicle without lawful authority on any road being a footpath, a bridleway or restricted byway. Road is defined as any highway and any other road to which the public has access[17]. By analogy to the position for a private right of way, which a landowner has lawful authority to grant, a public right of way could also arise from long user by the public; and use as of right could be evidence of dedication[18]. However, it is not open to a landowner to dedicate a vehicular route if to do so would cause a public nuisance to those using a public footpath[19].

2.7 **Towpaths** along canals or rivers are not public rights of way unless such rights have been dedicated either expressly or by long use[20]. If a right of way is dedicated, it will be subject to the primary need of navigation[21].

2.8 At common law there is no public right to walk on the **foreshore** (the land between medium high and medium low water). The rights of the public are limited to navigation and fishing. A public right of way may be dedicated expressly or by implication . The foreshore is generally owned by the Crown, which is not bound by s.31 of the Highways Act 1980 ('HA 1980'), so any claim to a deemed dedication over the foreshore would have to be made at common law[22]. In some instances, the Crown may have conveyed

---

16 WCA 1981, s.66(1).

17 Road Traffic Act 1988, s.192.

18 Bakewell Management Ltd v Brandwood [2004] 2 AC 519.

19 Hereford and Worcester County Council v Pick (1995) 71 P&CR 231.

20 Ball v Herbert (1789) 3 TR 253.

21 Grand Junction Canal Co v Petty (1888) 21 QBD 273.

22 As explained below in Section 3 at 3.10-3.20.

the foreshore to a local authority or the National Trust. As referred to below, the Marine and Coastal Access Act 2006 has introduced a new right of access to coastal areas.

**Long Distance Paths and Coastal Access**

2.9 Sections 50A-55 of the NPAC 1949 make provision for long-distance paths. It is now Natural England (having formerly been the National Parks Commission and then the Countryside Agency) which makes proposals for the route to the Secretary of State. These proposals may include new paths and ferries, where necessary, and may make provision for accommodation, meals and refreshments. If the Secretary of State gives his approval, highway authorities implement the proposals through creation agreements and orders and diversion orders.

2.10 The Marine and Coastal Access Act 2009 has amended the NPAC 1949 to enable a long-distance route to be established for the whole of the English coast, together with a margin of land in association with that route, accessible to the public for open-air recreation on foot. Where access is not available under other legislation, access rights under s.2(1) of the CROW 2000 will be applied.

## 3 CREATION OF PUBLIC RIGHTS OF WAY

3.1 Having identified the categories of public rights of way that exist and their characteristics, it is important to understand how they are created. This is by statute or by dedication and acceptance either at common law or by statutory presumption.

3.2 The HA 1980 is the main statute under which highways are now constructed. For roads, this is normally done by the highway authority acquiring the land by agreement or through the use of compulsory powers[23]. Highways constructed under these powers

[23] Part XII of the HA 1980 and the Acquisition of Land Act 1981.

and procedures become highways without the need for any dedication or acceptance.

3.3. Footpaths, bridleways and restricted byways however are usually created by agreements or orders or by dedication and acceptance[24].

## Public Path Creation Agreements

3.4 Footpaths, bridleways and restricted byways can be created by the landowner and the local authority[25]. The 'local authority' includes county councils and district councils. The meaning has been extended to include the Broads Authority and National Park authorities[26]. The local authority must have regard to the needs of agriculture (which includes the breeding and keeping of horses) and forestry and the desirability of conserving flora, fauna and geographical and physiographical features[27].

3.5 Once the agreement has been made, the local authority is obliged to take all necessary steps to ensure that the restricted byway, bridleway or footpath is dedicated in accordance with the agreement. The path becomes maintainable at public expense.

3.6 Parish and community councils also have power to enter into agreements for the creation of highways with those who have the

---

24 HA 1980, ss 25 & 26; Restricted Byways (Application and Consequential Amendment of Provisions) Regulations 2006 (S.I. 2006/1177).

25 HA 1980, s 25(1). Restricted Byways (Application and Consequential Amendment of Provisions) Regulations 2006 (SI 2006/1177).

26 HA 1980, s25(2); Norfolk and Suffolk Broads Act 1988, s 2(5) and (6), s 23(2) and Sch 3, para 47(1); Environment Act 1995, ss 70 and 125(2) and Sch 9, para 11(a0; Restricted Byways (Application and Consequential Amendment of Provisions) rRegaukltions2006 (SI 2006/1177).

27 HA 1980,s 29.

capacity to dedicate public rights of way over land in the parish or community or an adjoining parish or community[28].

## Public path Creation Orders

3.7 There is power under the HA 1980 for National Park authorities, district and county councils to make orders for the creation of footpaths, bridleways and restricted byways[29]. The power applies where it appears to the authority or council that there is a need for the new path, and it must be satisfied that it is expedient to create a new path. The Secretary of State may also make creation orders, subject to the same tests as apply to authorities. Compensation may be payable to landowners where the value of their land has been depreciated or suffered damage by being disturbed in the enjoyment of their land by the coming into effect of the creation order[30].

3.8 The procedure to be followed for making and confirming orders and for dealing with any objections is set out in the HA 1980[31]. The form of the Order is prescribed by regulations[32].

3.9 There is power for Natural England to make an application to the Secretary of State for a public path creation order to enable the public to obtain access, or to facilitate access, to access land under Part 1 of the CROW 2000. The application in Wales is made by the Natural Resources Body for Wales to the Welsh Minsters[33].

## Dedication and Acceptance

---

28 HA 1980, s 30.

29 HA 1980, s 26; Restricted Byways (Application and Consequential Amendment of Provisions) Regulations 2006 (SI 2006/1177).

30 HA 1980, s 28 and 307(1).

31 S 26(6) and Sch 6.

32 Public Path Orders Regulations 1993 (SI 1993/11), See Defra Rights of Way Circular 1/09, ' Guidance for Local Authorities' (2009).

33 CROW 2000, s 58(1).

3.10 Most new highways are now created under the statutory provisions referred to above. However, they can still be created by dedication at common law or under statute. Further, where there is any doubt over the nature and extent of public rights of way, an understanding of the applicable common law may in any event be necessary to establish whether these rights have been dedicated in the past.

3.11 Dedication can either be express or implied. An express dedication must be in perpetuity (i.e. forever) and therefore cannot be for a term of years[34]. The dedication may be limited, being subject, for example, to the right to hold fairs or markets, the provision of gates, or to allowing ploughing of a field[35]. Use by the public may be evidence of a dedicated route and also evidence of dedication itself. The use must be to a degree such that it would be obvious to the landowner that a route was being used by the public. There must be acceptance by the public of the dedication[36].

3.12 At common law, long use may give rise to an inferred dedication, with the onus being on the claimant to establish that the landowner dedicated the route as a public right of way[37]. It does not matter what the subjective belief of the users is in respect of their right or otherwise to use the land[38].

3.13 A statutory deemed dedication under section 31 of the HA 1980, arises where there has been 20 years' use before the right of way is brought into question and the onus is on the landowner to show that he had no intention to dedicate. However, at common law there is no specified period and the length of use that must be

---

34 Dawes v Hawkins (1860) 8 CB NS 848.

35 AG v Horner (1885) 11 App Cas 66.

36 R v Mellor (1830) 1 Lew CC 158; Cubitt v Maxse (1873) LR 8CP 704.

37 See e.g. Mann v Brodie (18850 10 App Cases 378, 386.

demonstrated depends upon all of the circumstances. In one case 18 months was held to be sufficient[39].

3.14 Whether in relation to inferred dedication under common law or deemed dedication under the HA 1980, the use relied on must be *as of right*. That is use which is *nec vi, nec clam* or *nec precario* which is:

(i) Peaceable and without force (e.g. breaking locks or fences) and is not contentious i.e. it has not been challenged by the landowner by, for example, a clearly worded and visible notice prohibiting access;

(ii) The use is not carried out secretly but openly, such that a landowner would be able to observe such use; and

(iii) It is without permission, which may be express or implied. Where a public right of way is recorded on a definitive map, whether correctly or in error, such use of that way will not be *as of right*. It is 'by right' by reason of the entry on the map. However, it does sometimes happen that an order to modify a definitive map is obtained but the authority overlook amending the definitive map (as explained in Section 4 below). In one such case, a claim for a public right of way over the original route was upheld on the basis of twenty years' use[40].

This acquisition of public rights is similar to the acquisition of a private right of way under the law of prescription. This approach also applies to the creation of a new village green, with which important analogies can be drawn[41].

---

38 As established by R v Oxfordshire County Council, ex parte Sunningwell Parish Council [2000] 1 AC 335.

39 North London Rail Company v St Mary, Islington Vestry (1827) 27 LT 672.

40 Powell v Irani v Secretary of State for the Environment, Food and Rural Affairs [2014] EWHC 4009 (Admin).

3.15 The dedication must be to the public at large and not to a class of persons, such as a path to a church which may be limited to the parishioners[42]. The acceptance, however, does not have to be by all members of the public, provided that the dedication has been accepted by a section of the public.

3.16 As long as the dedication is to the public at large, use only by local residents can be sufficient as long as there is nothing which prevented the route being used by any person[43]. Further, even if the original purpose of the route no longer exists (e.g. a route to specific facilities within a village or town which no longer exists) the right of way continues to have legal existence, provided that it was a genuine public right of way. There can be issues where the physical presence of a highway has ceased to exist, e.g. where there is a landslip (see below at 6.1).

3.17 However, dedication is required because mere use does not create a highway[44]. The burden rests on those claiming the right to demonstrate that it can be inferred from the landowner's conduct that he actually dedicated the route as a public right of way. If the evidence only shows tolerance by the landowner or lack of intention to dedicate, then use alone will not usually be sufficient[45].

3.18 Further, a landowner may have taken preventative measures to prevent the establishment of a right of way such as by putting up barriers, notices and turning people back or, and usually most effectively, lodging statements and declarations with the highways

41 In accordance with the Commons Act 2006, s 15. See R v Oxfordshire County Council, ex parte Sunningwell Parish Council [2000] 1 AC 335 for a clear explanation of the origin of prescriptive rights and their application to village greens.

42 *Highway Law* by Sauvain, Fifth edition, at 1-08 on p.4; *Public Rights of Way* by Sydenham, (2019) at 3.4.3 on p. 21.

43 R v Broke (1859) 1 F&F 514.

44 Attorney-General v Esher Linoleum Company Ltd. [1901] 2 Ch 647.

45 Folkstone Corporation v Brockman [1914] AC 338.

authority[46]. Shutting a path for at least one day a year has also been acknowledged as an accepted method of demonstrating no intention to dedicate[47]. It is not, however, sufficient for a landowner merely to state that he had no intention to dedicate[48].

3.19 Section 31 of the HA 1980 does not prevent reliance on the common law[49]. In particular this provision:

(i) Does not apply to the Crown, the Duchies of Lancaster and Cornwall, the Forestry Commission and government departments that count as the Crown.

(ii) Requires at least 20-years' use, as seen above. The use must have been used by the public as of right and without interruption for a full period of 20 years. Without interruption does not equate to continuous and is a question of fact. Interruption can arise from some actual and physical stopping of the use for example by placing a locked gate across the path.

(iii) There must be user *as of right* by the public at large and the absence of sufficient evidence of a lack of intention to dedicate. In contrast, at common law the person claiming the right has to show that the landowner intended or could be presumed to have intended, to dedicate a public right of way. Under section 31, it is for the landowner to rebut that presumption.

(iv) The use relied upon must immediately pre-date the event which brings the right of way into question. It may be

---

46 HA 1980, s.31(3) and (6) and see Burrows v Secretary of State for Environment, Food and Rural Affairs [2004] EWHC 132 (Admin) on the need for clarity in such notices.

47 Ali v Secretary of State for Environment, Food and Rural Affairs [2015] EWHC 893 (Admin).

48 Fairey v Southampton County Council [1956] 2 QB 439, 458.

49 HA 1980, s.31(9).

brought into question by e.g. a locked gate or notices inconsistent with a dedication of a public right of way.

3.20 It should be noted that the statutory presumption of dedication under s.31 cannot apply to land in the possession of a public body where such dedication would be incompatible with the public and statutory purposes for which the land is being held[50].

## 4 RECORDING OF PUBLIC RIGHTS OF WAY AND MODIFICATION ORDERS

4.1 As indicated above, footpaths and bridleways are not always obvious on the ground. Public rights of way are now, however, often marked with signs or coloured arrows, for example yellow for footpaths, blue for bridleways. They can be found on Ordnance Survey and other maps and on some council websites. However, the legal starting point to ascertain public rights of way in any area is the definitive map and statement for that area.

### The requirement to prepare a definitive map and statement

4.2 The NPAC 1949 required the highways authorities to undertake a survey of the public paths within their area and to prepare a map of the paths, to be known as the "definitive map and statement", as referred to above. Originally the paths mapped included three categories:

(a) Footpaths;

(b) Bridleways; and

---

[50] Regarding a discussion and application of the statutory incompatibility principle see the village green cases of R (on the application of Newhaven Port and Properties Ltd) v East Sussex CC [2015] A.C. 1547 and R (on the application of Lancashire CC) v Secretary of State for the Environment, Food and Rural Affairs [2020] 2 W.L.R 1.

(c) Roads used as a public path" ("RUPPs"). These were defined as highways, other than public paths, used by the public mainly for the purposes for which footpaths and bridleways are so used.[51] It was uncertain whether there were rights for vehicles or not, which led to some confusion and reclassification and ultimately the re-designation of RUPPS.[52]

4.3 The procedure set out under the NPAC 1949 was modified and simplified by the Countryside Act 1968 and the WCA 1981 then modified the procedure for the preparation and revision of definitive maps. As seen above (at 2.5(c) and (d)), RUPPS have been re-designated as restricted byways and there are also BOATs which term was introduced by the Countryside Act 1968.

## The significance and limitations of a definitive map and statement

4.4 The definitive map and statement records public rights of way. It is conclusive of the rights recorded, albeit when certain events take place the recorded rights may be altered, deleted or added to, as outlined below, by modification of the map and statement. The definitive map and statement is maintained by the surveying authority. Other authorities, including town and parish councils, should also have a copy of that part of the definitive map which covers their area and any orders which have been made amending the map and statement. It should be available for inspection at all reasonable hours and free of charge[53]. Some but not all authorities enable online access to the definitive map, which of course has been particularly helpful during the restrictions that have closed some Council offices at time during the Covid-19 pandemic.

4.5 However, although conclusive of the recorded rights, there may be valid rights of way which are not recorded in the definitive

[51] NPAC 1949, s.27(2).

[52] By the Countryside Act 1968 and CROW 2000 respectively.

[53] WCA 1981, s 57.

map and statement or there could be errors in the details of those that are recorded. There may for example be public path orders that have been confirmed but not recorded on the map; definitive map orders and public path orders may have been made, but not confirmed; there may be applications for such map or path modification orders; there may be documentary evidence of the valid existence of public rights of way not recorded; and there may be user evidence which would support an application to make a definitive map order (as addressed below) without an application having yet been made.

4.6 Further, the details in the definitive map and statement may not fit with the position on the ground. The small scale of most definitive maps is such that the route on the ground may not be shown with sufficient accuracy or clarity. Sometimes the position is clarified by the definitive statement, although care may be needed in interpreting the statement. Further, where there is a real conflict between the statement and the map, it is likely that the map will prevail[54].

## The duties of the surveying authority

4.7 The duties are set out in Part III of the WCA 1981. The Deregulation Act 2015 when in force will amend Part III and make several important changes to the surveying authorities' duties with the aim of introducing in England a streamlined procedure for updating the definitive map in response to applications made for modification orders. However, as these changes are not in force, this section relates to the law as it currently remains.

4.8 The purpose of the legislation is to ensure that public rights of way are properly identified and do not disappear through non-use. The surveying authority is under a duty to keep the map up to date and under continuous review. The authority may make

---

54 R (Norfolk County Council) v Secretary of State for the Environment Food and Rural Affairs [2005] EWHC 119 at [38], [64] and [73].

modification orders in compliance with the statutory provisions of its own volition, in response to an application having been made or being legally required to make such an order[55].

4.9 The authority must take into account events before the coming into effect of the WCA 1981 as well as subsequent events and the authority must, as soon as practicable after the occurrence of the specified events in s.53(3)(a), make by order such modifications to the map and statement as appear to them to be necessary as a consequence of the occurrence of that event[56]. These are legal event orders, with the specified events required to be reflected in the definitive map and statement being threefold:

(i) Where the highway has been authorised to be stopped up, diverted, widened or extended, usually under the HA 1980.

(ii) Where for example greater rights over a footpath or bridleway are created by agreement or order, or where the path has been downgraded as a result of an order.

(iii) Where a new right (a footpath or bridleway) has been created either by agreement or by order.

4.10 Further, any person may apply for an order under s.53(3)(b) and (c):

(1) S.53(3)(b) applies where there is a claimed dedication of a public path or a bridleway by reason of enjoyment by the public during the required period.

(2) S.53(3)(c) relates to where there has been discovery by the authority of evidence which shows:

(i) that a right of way not shown in the definitive map and statement subsists or is reasonably alleged to subsist over land in the area being a public path, a restricted byway or a byway open to all traffic;

55 WCA 1981, s.53.

56 WCA 1981, s.53(2)(a).

(ii) that a highway shown in the map and statement should be of a different description to that shown; or

(iii) that there is no public right of way over land which is shown in the map and statement as a highway of any description, or any other particulars contained in the map and statement require modification.

4.11 In terms of section 53(3)(c), this is concerned with the correction of mistakes in the definitive map and statement and covers errors of inclusion of paths as well as of omission. Further, a path may be "upgraded" from a path of lower status (i.e. of more limited rights) to one of higher status or "downgraded" from a path of higher status to one of lower status[57]. The 'discovery' of evidence has been held to relate to the finding of some information which was previously unknown but also may relate to information which may or may not have existed at the time the definitive map was prepared or last updated.

4.12 The procedure for applying for, making, objecting to and confirming these orders is provided for in Schedule 14 to the WCA 1981and regulations[58]. The details are outside the scope of this Chapter. As referred to above, the Deregulation Act 2015 when in force will amend the procedure and introduce a new Schedule 13A in England replacing Schedule 14 to the WCA 1981. This introduces a new preliminary assessment procedure. However, Schedule 14 will still apply to Wales.

4.13 Before making an order, the authority has to comply with the publicity and consultation requirements. The authority may confirm a public path order or a definitive map order if no relevant objections have been made. However, where there are such objections, the order has to be referred to the Secretary of State for confirmation, modification or refusal. These objections will be

57 See e.g. *Highway Law* by Sauvain (Fifth edition) at 12-53 on p.466.

58 Wildlife and Countryside (Definitive Maps and Statements) Regulations 1993 (SI 1993/12).

considered by an independent Inspector by way of written representations or at a hearing or public inquiry, to which the Rights of Way (Hearing and Inquiry Procedure) (England) Rules 2007 (SI 2007/2008) apply. The Planning Inspectorate provide very comprehensive and helpful guidance on both the making of such orders and the procedure to be used and the relevant factors in deciding whether to confirm the order[59].

4.14 If the Inspector confirms the order, an application may be made to the High Court challenging the decision on the basis that it is not within the power of the Inspector or that there has been a procedural irregularity and, as a consequence, the claimant's interests have been substantially prejudiced. Any such application must be made within 42 days of the decision being published in the newspaper and cannot otherwise be challenged[60].

4.15 Where the Inspector refuses to confirm the order there is no statutory right to challenge that decision but an application may be made for permission to judicially review the decision under Part 54 of the Civil Procedure Rules. Such an application has to be filed with the Court Office promptly or in any event within 3 months of the decision. Judicial review is limited to a point of law and not a re-run of the merits of the order and the evidence.

---

[59] Guidance on procedures for considering objections to definitive map and public path orders in England (October 2018). See also the Planning Inspectorate's Rights of Way Section Advice Notes and Defra's Circular 1/09 (October 2009); Guidance for Local Authorities.

[60] HA 1980, Sch 2, para. 4; WCA 1981, Sch 15, para 12. For a recent example of such a challenge with a discussion of the principles applicable to such challenges see Garland v Secretary of State for Environment, Food and Rural Affairs [2020] EWHC 1814 (Admin).

## 5 MAINTENANCE AND PROTECTION OF PUBLIC PATHS AND RESTRICTED BYWAYS

### Ownership of the land

5.1 Owners and occupiers of land crossed by a public right of way must keep the route visible and not obstruct or endanger users. Where the public right of way is publicly maintainable, the surface is vested in the highway authority for highway purposes. The landowner is allowed to use the right of way for his own purposes provided that this does not interfere with the rights of the public or disturb the surface of the way. The landowner usually retains an interest in the subsoil and the airspace above.

5.2 Where a highway is not publicly maintainable, the landowner retains the legal interest in the whole of the land. However, the owner may not construct buildings over or under the highway without the consent of the highway authority.

5.3 Where a right of way separates land in different ownership, there is a rebuttable presumption that the adjoining landowner owns the land up to the centre point of the way adjoining the property (*usque ad medium filum*).

### Liability for maintenance and repairs

5.4 With regard to who is liable for maintaining a highway, this can be complex. A landowner may be liable under a local or private Act of Parliament, or, and much less commonly, liability may have arisen by prescription where liability has existed from time immemorial.

5.5 Liability for repairs is generally treated as resting with the highway authority, unless the authority can prove otherwise[61].

---

61 Attorney-General v Watford Road District Council [1912] 1 Ch 417.

## Interference with use of a public right of way

5.6 Part IX of the HA 1980 deals with the lawful and unlawful interference with highways including protection of public rights, damage to highways, obstruction of highways and damage or annoyance to users of highways.

5.7 Any person who without lawful authority or excuse wilfully obstructs a highway is guilty of an offence under the HA 1980, s.137 and is liable to pay a fine. Further, on the conviction of a person for the wilful obstruction of a highway a magistrates' court may, in addition to or in place of a fine, order that person to remove the obstruction within a specified time, provided that person has power to do so[62]. Failure to comply with such an order is punishable by a fine and if the offence is continued there can be a fine for each day the offence is continued. Further, a highway authority can remove an obstruction following conviction and recover the expenses of so doing from the convicted person.

5.8 Where vegetation overhangs the side of a path and obstructs the passage of vehicles or pedestrians or endangers or obstructs the passage of a horse, the highway authority may serve a notice on the owner of the tree, shrub or hedge, or on the occupier of the land on which it is growing, requiring the cutting back or lopping of the vegetation so as to remove the cause of danger[63]. If the works are not carried out in accordance with the notice, the authority can do the work itself and recover the expenses. Any person aggrieved by such a notice may appeal to the magistrates' court.

5.9 Gates and other structures (e.g. stiles, cattle grids, fences and wires) can be lawfully be placed across a public right of way if the path was originally dedicated subject to then. The definitive statement should record any such limitation on the dedication. If

---

62 HA 1980, s.137ZA inserted by the CROW 2000, s.64.

63 HA 1980, s.154.

not authorised, they would amount to an obstruction. A statutory notice may also be served by the authority on the occupier requiring removal of unauthorised structures[64]. If the occupier fails to comply with the notice and remove the structure, the authority may do so itself and recover its reasonable expenses.

5.10 Gates which are authorised are required to be of a minimum width – for a bridleway that is 5 feet; for a carriageway including a BOAT, the minimum width is 10 feet[65]. It is the duty of the landowner to maintain any stile, gate or other structure across a footpath, bridleway or restricted byway[66]. Further, there is power for a highway authority to authorise the erection of stiles, gates or other works across a footpath or bridleway on land that is being brought into use for agriculture in order to prevent the ingress or egress of animals[67]. The maintenance of any such structure so authorised will be in accordance with the conditions imposed on the authorisation.

5.11 If a responsible landowner does not maintain a stile, gate or other structure in a safe condition and to the standard of repair required to prevent unreasonable interference with the rights of persons using the footpath, bridleway, restricted byway or BOAT, the authority or district council may, after giving 14 days' notice, enter and do the work and recover the cost[68].

5.12 Where electric or barbed wire fences are erected along the side of a path, that may amount to a public nuisance, especially if members of the public are likely to wander into the fence. A

---

64 HA 1980, s.143.

65 HA 1980, s.145.

66 HA 1980, s.146.

67 HA 1980, s.147.

68 HA 1980, s.146(2).

barbed wire fence can be the subject of a statutory notice to remove it[69].

5.13 The is also power for the highway authority or district council to enter into an agreement with the owner, lessee or occupier of land relating to improvements for the benefit of those with mobility problems[70].

5.14 The ploughing of fields can interfere with the exercise of a public right of way. A right of way may have been dedicated subject to the right to plough, and if so, this may be recorded in the definitive statement. In the absence of such a record, the farmer may try to rely upon a common law right to plough. Even without that, there is a statutory right under section162 of the HA 1980 which applies to cross-field footpaths and bridleways over agricultural land. That right only applies where it is not reasonably convenient to avoid ploughing or disturbing the surface when sowing or cultivating a crop and after ploughing or other disturbance the surface must be made good to at least the minimum width and within the specified period. There is no statutory right to plough field-edge paths.

5.15 It is an offence for any person to place or maintain on or near any footpath, bridleway or restricted byway shown on a definitive map a notice containing a false or misleading statement likely to deter the public from using the way[71].

5.16 There are special provisions in the WCA 1981 relating to bulls. It is an offence for the occupier of a field crossed by a footpath, bridleway, restricted byway or BOAT to keep a bull in a field. This is subject to various qualifications regarding the age of the bull and the breed. The health and safety executive insist on a warning

---

69 HA 1980, s. 164.

70 HA 1980, s.147ZA introduced by CROW 2000, s.69 and also HA 1980, s.175A

71 NPAC 1949, s.57

notice (e.g. "Bull in field") being displayed when a bull is present in a field.

## 6 DIVERSIONS AND EXTINGUISHMENTS

6.1 Even where a highway has not been used for many years and may not be visible on the ground, its legal existence continues until a statutory procedure is used to either change its position or to extinguish it. Part VIII of the HA 1980 sets out the powers in relation to the stopping up and diversion of highways. This reflects the old saying of "Once a highway, always a highway", and so there is the need for express powers where any change in those highway rights is proposed[72]. This may, however, not apply where the highway has ceased to exist physically, as for example where a cliff, on which a footpath previously ran, falls into the sea[73].

6.2 Restricted byways, bridleways and footpaths may be stopped up (extinguished) by an order under s.118 of the HA 1980 which provides that where it appears to a council that it is expedient to do so on the ground that it is not needed for public use they may make the order which has to be confirmed by the Secretary of State. In making the order the authority must have regard to the needs of agriculture, forestry and nature conservation[74]. The procedure for the making, confirmation, validity and date of operation of public path extinguishment orders is provided for in Schedule 6 to the HA 1980. Further, there can be concurrent orders involving creation and diversion orders and extinguishment orders[75]. In making and confirming an extinguishment

---

72 Harvey v Truro RDC [1902] 2 Ch 638.

73 Although there is now provisions for 'roll back' of the long-distance trail under the Marine and Coastal Access Act 2009, s.302 which introduces a new s.55B into the NPAC 1949. See Public Rights of Way by Sydenham (2019) at Section 6, p.59.

74 HA 1980, ss.121(3) and 29, as amended by CROW 2000, Sch 6, Pt I, para 14(4).

75 HA 1980, s.118(5).

order, the local authority or Secretary of State may have regard to the extent to which the public path creation order or the public path diversion order would provide an alternative path.

6.3 There is also power to apply to the magistrates' court under section 116 of the HA 1980 to stop up or divert a highway on the basis that:

(i) It is unnecessary; or

(ii) It can be diverted so as to make it nearer or more commodious to the public.

Unlike section 118, section 116 can be used to extinguish rights for mechanically propelled vehicles subject to the reservation of a restricted byway, bridleway or footpath rights. Provided the appropriate test can be fulfilled, a bridleway could be extinguished and, concurrently, a new right created for walkers[76].

6.4 The council has power to make a diversion order under section 119 of the HA 1980 where in respect of a footpath, bridleway or restricted byway it appears to them that in the interests of the owner, lessee or occupier of land crossed by the path or way, it is expedient that the line of the path, or part of that line, should be diverted. As for an extinguishment order, the procedure is for an order to be made and then confirmed. Where there are objections, the order must be referred to the Secretary of State for confirmation. Anyone whose property can be shown to have been adversely affected by a public path order under the HA 1980, may be able to claim compensation[77].

6.5 There are also specific powers under Part X of the TCPA 1990 for the diversion and extinguishment of public rights of way to enable development pursuant to a planning permission to be

---

[76] HA 1980, s.26 – see Public Rights of Way by Sydenham (2019) at 6.3.1 on p. 61.

[77] HA 1980, ss. 121(2) and 28. Also for the practicalities of making a public path order see Public Rights of Way by Sydenham (20019) at 6.6.6 on pp.72-74.

carried out. This is outside the scope of this Chapter but is usefully summarised in *Public Rights of Way* by Sydenham (2019)[78].

[78] Section 6.6 on p.74.

# CHAPTER EIGHT

# OTHER ACCESS RIGHTS IN THE NATIONAL PARKS

*Stephen Whale and Jacqueline Lean*

## 1 INTRODUCTION

1.1 It is said that almost half the common land in England is in National Parks, and that it comprises nearly 20% of the area of the National Parks in England (if one includes common land in the New Forest National Park).[1] It is also said that common land accounts for approximately 8.5% of land in Wales, some of which is in National Parks.[2] This Chapter discusses the rights of common (Section 2), and (in Section 3) the evolution of access rights to common land before the advent of the Countryside and Rights of Way Act 2000 ("the CROW 2000"), including the powers of NPAs to enter into access agreements under the 1949 Act. Section 4 discusses the "right to roam" introduced by the CROW 2000 and the powers of NPAs under that Act as access authorities. The Chapter concludes with a brief overview of the rights and liabilities of owners in relation to access land (Section 5).

## 2 COMMON LAND

2.1 There are two habitual misconceptions regarding "common land". The first is that it is in some form of public ownership. On the contrary, most common land is privately owned. The second is that the public has a right of access to all of it. This position remains inaccurate, although the CROW 2000 (discussed later in this chapter) has done much to alter the position. These misconceptions owe much to the long and complex history of common land, and to the combination of common law and statute law pertaining to it.

---

1 *Gadsden & Cousins on Commons and Greens* (Sweet & Maxwell, 3rd ed., 2020) at 11-17. This work is commended as a detailed work on the law of commons and greens. As for the New Forest (and Dartmoor), see below.

2 *Ibid.*, at 17-01.

## Definition of common land

2.2 As a general definition, "common land" can be described as land over which a right of common may be exercised. A right of common is the legal right of a person (a "commoner") to take or use some part of the natural produce of the land of another person. Rights of common are in the nature of *profits à prendre*, and a species of incorporeal hereditaments. The natural produce of the land not taken or used by the commoner belongs to the owner of the soil of the common land. Most common land is unenclosed, but that is not to say that it must be unenclosed. It follows that the physical nature of land is no necessary indication of its legal status as common land or otherwise.

2.3 There is no single definition of common land at common law, and indeed the common law recognises a range of classes of common land (or similar). By the same token, there is a range of definitions in statute. For present purposes, a useful reference is the definition in section 22(1) of the Commons Registration Act 1965. Thus:

> *"(1) In this Act, unless the context otherwise requires, "common land" means –*
>
> *land subject to rights of common (as defined in this Act) whether those rights are exercisable at all times or only during limited periods;*
>
> *waste land of a manor not subject to rights of common;*
>
> *but does not include a town or village green or any land which forms part of a highway."*

2.4 It can be seen that Parliament elected to include within the definition a category of land, namely waste land of a manor, even though not subject to rights of common.

2.5 Section 1 of the CROW 2000 does not include a definition of "common land", although it does include in subsection (3) a definition of "registered common land" for the purposes of Part I. This is of significance because of the definition of "access land" in subsection (1). However, note Schedule 5 paragraph 7 to the Commons Act 2006. This amends the subsection (3) definition, but it is at present only partially in force.

2.6 The Commons Act 2006 does not include a definition of "common land" either, although see section 61(2)(a) on land registered as common land.

## Rights of common

2.7 Rights of common are many and various, although they have traditionally been divided into six categories: common in the soil, estovers, pannage, pasturage, piscary and turbary. It should also be mentioned that the courts have accepted that the right to take and carry away wild animals (animals *ferae naturae*) may exist as a right of common.[3]

2.8 As its name suggests, "common in the soil" is the right to take part of the soil (or minerals) from the common land. The meanings of other categories, with the possible exception of pasturage, are not self-evident. In simple terms "estovers" is a right to take timber. The term "pannage" connotes a right to graze pigs on fallen acorns or beech-mast in woodlands or forests, usually in the autumn.[4] The right of "pasturage" is the right to take grass by the mouths of cattle. The common of "piscary" is the right to take fish from a pond, lake, stream or river, the bed of which belongs to someone other than the commoner. A common of "turbary" is the right to take turf or peat for burning as fuel.

---

3 For a fascinating discussion of the classification of animals in English law and the nature of proprietary rights in relation to animals, amongst other issues, see Borwick Development Solutions Limited v Clear Water Fisheries Limited [2020] EWCA Civ 578. The case concerns fish in nine enclosed lakes, from which they cannot escape. It is not a rights of common case.

4 The time of pannage in the New Forest is a period of not less than 60 consecutive days as may be fixed annually by the Forestry Commissioners after consultation with the verderers: section 7 New Forest Act 1964.

2.9 It is to be observed that these six (or seven) categories of rights of common have nothing to do with access rights, save to the extent to which the commoner (or commoners) in question has an associated right to enter the common land in order to exercise their particular right or rights of common.

## 3 THE EVOLUTION OF PUBLIC ACCESS RIGHTS TO COMMON LAND BEFORE THE COUNTRYSIDE AND RIGHTS OF WAY ACT 2000

3.1 The roots of common land of the kind under consideration can be traced back to the feudal system imposed after the Norman Conquest and the subsequent development of the manorial system. A stepping stone along the way to today's system of public access to common land was the Restriction on Building Act 1592, which required the preservation of common or waste land within three miles of the cities of London and Westminster for recreational use by the public. It is also to be observed that there was, historically, *de facto* public access to much common land even if there was not, strictly, a right of public access.

3.2 However, punctuating the 1592 Act and today's system of public access to common land was the enclosure movement. This movement is associated both with the physical enclosure of land, using walls, fences and hedges, and with the legal inclosure of land whereby the rights of non-owners (including rights of common) were removed. One effect of the enclosure movement was to reduce *de facto* and legal rights of access to large swathes of land, an effect which in some quarters has been lamented down the ages and which has helped inspire the periodic actions and changes towards today's system.[5]

3.3 Those changes included the various Metropolitan Commons Acts between 1866 and 1898, which served to put a break on further inclosure. Whilst they did not afford public access to metro-

[5] For a poignant lament, see *Remembrances* (1832) by the poet John Clare.

politan commons as such, schemes made pursuant to these Acts conferred management powers and regulated public access. It has been said that these schemes probably created a statutory trust for the land to be managed for public recreation.[6] These Victorian Acts were quickly followed by the Commons Act 1899, Part I of which provides for the making of schemes in the prescribed form for the regulation, management and improvement of commons. By virtue of Schedule 9 paragraph 1 to the Environment Act 1995, NPAs have a qualified power to make these schemes in relation to a "registered common".[7] The Conservation Boards of the Cotswolds and Chilterns Areas of Outstanding Natural Beauty have also been afforded the power to make such schemes. The prevailing model scheme states as follows with respect to public access:

> "*The inhabitants of the neighbourhood shall have a right of free access to every part of the common…*"[8]

3.4 The Open Spaces Act 1906 and the Commons Act 1908 are of limited if any application to the areas of land under consideration in this chapter and book, but the same cannot be said for the Law of Property Act 1925 ("the 1925 Act") and its section 193 in particular.[9] Subject to provisos, this affords members of the public with "rights of access for air and exercise" to the metropolitan commons as well as to land which is "manorial waste, or a common, which is wholly or partly situated within an area which immediately before 1st April 1974 was a borough or urban district, and to any land which at the commencement of this Act is subject to rights of common and to which this section may from time to time be applied."[10] It should not be thought that the reference to borough and urban districts necessarily precludes the

---

6 *Gadsden & Cousins* at 9-28.

7 The relevant definition of "common" is found in section 15 of the 1899 Act.

8 Commons (Schemes) Regulations 1982, SI 1982/209. The predecessor prescribed schemes have all included very similar wording.

9 As amended.

application of this provision to rural areas. Indeed, it applies to large areas of the Lake District and South Wales.[11]

3.5 In R v Secretary of State for the Environment, Transport and the Regions, ex parte Billson [1999] Q.B. 374, the then owner had applied section 193 to Ranmore Common in Surrey by an expressly revocable deed dated 12 December 1929. Decades later, an appointed Inspector decided not to confirm an order modifying the definitive map and statement on the grounds that the user of certain tracks had not been "as of right" given the 1929 deed. The High Court upheld the Inspector's conclusion. In so doing, Sullivan J (as he then was) held that Parliament had intended in 1925 "to confer the broadest possible rights of access for air and exercise" to the qualifying commons, subject only to the limitations set out in paragraphs (a)-(d) of the proviso to section 193(1), and that these rights included access on horseback.

3.6 One adjunct to the rights afforded by section 193(1) is the criminal offence created by section 193(4). The enforcement mechanism previously found in section 194 of the 1925 Act has been replaced by the enforcement mechanism in section 41 of the Commons Act 2006.

3.7 A further impetus towards today's system of public access to common land was provided by the mass trespass of Kinder Scout, in the Peak District,[12] on 24 April 1932. Accounts of the event

[10] The Act came into force on 1 January 1926, but section 193(1) is worded in such a way that it applies to land becoming a qualifying common after that date. Note also subsection (2), repealed in Wales but not in England, by which the lord of the manor or other person entitled to the soil of any land subject to rights of common may by deed declare that section 193 shall apply to the land.

[11] Explanatory notes to the CROW 2000, paragraph 7, prepared by the Department of the Environment, Transport and the Regions with the Office of the Secretary of State for Wales.

[12] Nineteen years later, the Peak District became England's first National Park. Kinder Scout plateau includes its highest point.

vary, but the generally accepted account is one of several hundred walkers trespassing on the plateau in order to draw attention to the fact that general public access to areas of open country in private ownership was denied. There were scuffles with game-keepers, who resisted the trespass on behalf of the landowners, and some of the walkers were convicted of violent offences. The event led directly to the Access to Mountains Act 1939 and, ultimately, to the National Parks and Access to the Countryside Act 1949 ("the 1949 Act").[13] It has been said that the former "has been ridiculed for the most part as a capitulation to landed interests", but that its achievement "was to ratchet forward both ramblers' expectations and a greater preparedness on the part of landed interests to provide the recreational opportunity anticipated by a post-war, largely urban population."[14]

3.8 The early post-War period saw the enactment of the 1949 Act. Section 59(1) renders the provisions of its Part V effective for enabling the public to have access for open-air recreation to "open country" (as defined in subsection (2)), to which the provisions of section 60 are applied by an "access agreement" or by an "access order", or which is acquired for the purpose of giving to the public access thereto.

3.9 Subject to the provisos in the balance of Part V, and by virtue of section 60(1), where an access agreement or order is in force as respects any land a person who enters upon land comprised in the agreement or order for the purpose of open-air recreation without breaking or damaging any wall, fence, hedge or gate, or who is on such land for that purpose after having so entered thereon, "shall not be treated as a trespasser on that land or incur any other liability by reason only of so entering or being on the land". It follows that anyone entering qualifying land by breaking or dam-

13 For an interesting discussion of the mass trespass of Kinder Scout, the creation of the National Parks and the "right to roam" campaign, see *22 Ideas that Saved the English Countryside* (Frances Lincoln Limited, 2016).

14 Abstract of *The Access to Mountains Act 1939*, John Sheail, Rural History Vol. 21 Issue 1 (Cambridge University Press, 5 March 2010).

aging any wall, fence, hedge or gate is liable to an action in trespass. Moreover, Schedule 2 paragraph 1 to the 1949 Act provides that section 60(1) shall not apply to a person who, in or upon the land in question, engages in activity within one of the 15 categories set out. Some of these activities (drives or rides any vehicle, lights any fire, takes any dog not under proper control, leaves any litter) are unsurprising; others (disturbs any fish, writes any notice, delivers any political address) are somewhat surprising. Engaging in any of the proscribed activities also gives rise to liability for an action in trespass.

3.10 One proviso is that section 60(1) shall not apply to land which for the time being is "excepted land" (as defined in subsection (5)). The meaning of excepted land in the 1949 Act is similar to, but not identical to, the meaning in section 1 of the CROW 2000 (discussed later in this chapter). It is worth mentioning that the definition in the 1949 Act includes land to which section 193 of the Law of Property Act 1925 (discussed above) for the time being applies.

3.11 Pursuant to section 64(1)-(2) of the 1949 Act, LPAs (which includes for this purpose the National Park Authorities and the Conservation Boards for the Cotswolds and Chilterns Areas of Outstanding Natural Beauty) may make an access agreement with any person having an interest in land, being open country, in the authority's area. It may provide for the making of payments by the authority of either or both of the following descriptions, that is to say in consideration of the making of the agreement and by way of contribution towards expenditure incurred by the person making the agreement in consequence thereof. Access agreements can be irrevocable or subject to such provisions for revocation or variation as may be specified in the agreement.[15]

3.12 Section 65 of the 1949 Act affords LPAs power to make an access order, subject to Ministerial confirmation, as an alternative to an access agreement. The provisions in that behalf of the First

15 See subsection (3).

Schedule to the 1949 Act apply to the making, confirmation, coming into operation and validity of access orders.[16] Before making an access order in respect of land in a National Park, the LPA must consult with Natural England or the Natural Resources Body for Wales, as the case may be.[17] Where it appears desirable to the relevant consultee that such an order should be made in respect of land in a National Park, it may request the LPA to make an order accordingly. Section 90 of the 1949 Act affords LPAs power to make byelaws with respect to land to which the public are given access by an agreement or order, or in consequence of acquisition, under Part V.

3.13 Opinion varies as to the effectiveness of access agreements and orders. Some 50,000 hectares of access land are thought to have been secured under the 1949 Act,[18] although it is not necessarily the case that much or all of it is common land. There are no known confirmed access orders relating to common land. Access orders and agreements have been described as "largely a dead letter".[19] Section 46(2) of the CROW 2000, not yet in force, precludes new access agreements or orders under Part V of the 1949 Act in relation to land which is open country or registered common land for the purposes of Part I of the 2000 Act.

3.14 Section 19(1) of the Ancient Monuments and Archaeological Areas Act 1979 affords the public a right of access (subject to the remaining provisions of section 19) to any monument under the

---

16 See subsection (4).

17 See subsections (5)-(5A). This section of this chapter, on access to common land, is concerned only with land in England and Wales. One result of devolution is that the statutory provisions with respect to each are increasingly divergent. Readers are encouraged always to double-check the statutory provisions applicable to England or Wales, as the case may be.

18 Explanatory notes to the Countryside and Rights of Way Act 2000, paragraph 7, prepared by the Department of the Environment, Transport and the Regions with the Office of the Secretary of State for Wales.

19 *A Legal History of the English Landscape*, Christopher Jessel (Wildy, Simmonds & Hill Publishing, 2011), at page 183.

ownership or guardianship of the Secretary of State, the Historic Buildings and Monuments Commission for England or a local authority by virtue of the 1979 Act. Those remaining provisions include the power to control the times of normal public access and even entirely to exclude the public from access for such period as the relevant owner or guardian thinks fit. There are also powers to charge for admission and to refuse admission. There is no reason why section 19 cannot apply to common land.

3.15 There is a wide range of local or private Acts affording public rights of access to common land, with implications for some public Acts and land within National Parks. For example, neither sections 1-10 of the Commons Registration Act 1965 nor Part 1 of the Commons Act 2006 applies to the New Forest.[20] Subject to provisos, section 10 of the Dartmoor Commons Act 1985 affords the public a right of access to "the commons"[21] on foot and on horseback for the purpose of open-air recreation. There is a cross-reference in subsection (3) of the same to certain provisions of the 1949 Act.

3.16 The various public rights of access to common land discussed above continue to have ongoing relevance, despite the CROW 2000, not least because of section 1(1) of the 2000 Act. This excludes, from the definition of "access land" in Part I, land which is treated by section 15(1) as being accessible to the public apart from the 2000 Act. There are four categories of land in section 15(1), which can be summarised as: land to which section 193 of the Law of Property Act 1925 applies; land to which members of the public have a right of access at all times for the purposes of open-air recreation by virtue of a local or private Act or a scheme made under Part I of the Commons Act 1899; land to which an access agreement or order under Part V of the 1949 Act is in force; and land to which the public have or would have

20 See section 11(1) of the Commons Registration Act 1965 and section 5(2)(a) of the Commons Act 2006, respectively.

21 Defined in section 2(1).

access under section 19 of the Ancient Monuments and Archaeological Areas Act 1979.

3.17 It is the "right to roam" under the CROW 2000 to which this chapter now turns.

## 4 THE "RIGHT TO ROAM"

4.1 The "right to roam" was introduced by Part 1 of the CROW 2000. Contrary to its colloquial name, and indeed the pre-amble to the Act,[22] Part 1 of CROW 2000 does not confer a free-standing general right of "access" to or 'roaming of' the countryside. It does, however, confer a right for members of the public to enter onto, and remain on, "access land" for the purposes of recreation, subject to certain restrictions and conditions.

### Definition of access land

4.2 "Access land" is defined in s.1 of CROW 2000. S.1 is in slightly different terms in respect of land in England and in Wales, but "access land" broadly comprises:

i Any land shown as "open country" on a map in conclusive form[23] issued by Natural England (for land in England) or by the Natural Resources Body for Wales (for land in Wales)[24]. "Open country" is defined[25] as land which appears to Natural England / the Natural Resources Body for Wales to consist wholly or predominantly of mountain,

[22] Which commences, "An Act to make new provision for public access to the countryside..."

[23] I.e. a map prepared under the provisions of ss4-10 of CROW 2000.

[24] S.1(1)(a)

[25] In s.1(2)

moor, heath or down[26] and is not registered common land, coastal margin or (in England) land dedicated under section 16 CROW 2000;

ii Any land which is situated more than 600m above sea level in any area for which no such map has been issued[27];

iii Land shown on such a map as registered common land[28];

iv Registered common land in any area outside Inner London for which no such map relating to registered common land has been issued[29];

v Land which is "coastal margin" – i.e. land of a description specified by an Order made under s.3A CROW 2000; and

vi Land dedicated under s.16 CROW 2000 for the purpose of Part 1 of the Act, but not including

---

26 Those terms are also defined in s.1(2). "Mountain" is defined as including land more than 600m above sea level, but, importantly, land does not fall within a definition of "mountain, moor, heath or down" if it appears to Natural England / the Natural Resources Body for Wales to consist of "improved or semi-improved grassland".

27 S.1(1)(d). "Registered common land" is defined in s.1(3)-(4). By way of summary, "registered common land" comprises (a) land registered under the Commons Act 1965 whose registration under that Act has become final, or (b) land falling within (a) on or after the date CROW 2000 was passed but which has subsequently ceased to be registered under that Act by reason of the register on which it was included having been amended by reason of the land ceasing to be common land within the meaning of that Act. Land does not fall within (b) where the amendment of the register was made pursuant to an application made before CROW 2000 was passed; or where the land has ceased to be common land by reason of the exercise of powers of compulsory purchase or of appropriation or of sale conferred by an enactment, or any power so conferred under which land may be made common land (within the meaning of the Commons Act 1965) in substitution for other land.

28 S.1(1)(b)

29 S.1(1)(c)

"excepted land"[30] or land which is treated by s.15(1) as being accessible to the public apart from the provisions of CROW 2000.

4.3 Under s.3A CROW 2000, the Secretary of State may, by order, specify descriptions of land in England which are "coastal margin" for the purposes of the Act. This section was inserted by the Marine and Coastal Act 2009, as part of the (then) Government's commitment towards improving public access to the coastline.[31] The descriptions of land specified as coastal margin are set out in paragraph 3 of The Access to the Countryside (Coastal Margin) Order 2010. A power is conferred on Welsh Ministers under s.3 to extend the definition of "open country" in s.(1) to include coastal land, or coastal land of any description. That power has not, as yet, been exercised.

4.4 Under s.16 CROW 2000, a landowner – being the person who holds the fee simple absolute in possession, or a legal term of years absolute of not less than 90 years – may dedicate land as access land (and, where appropriate, as coastal margin). The procedure for doing so is set out in the Access to the Countryside (Dedication of Land) (England) Regulations 2003 and the Access to the Countryside (Dedication of Land as Access Land) (Wales)

---

30 I.e land of a description falling within any of the descriptions specified in Part 1 of Schedule 1 of CROW 2000 (those descriptions having effect subject to Part 2 of Schedule 1).

31 Part 9 of the Marine and Coastal Access Act 2009 places a duty on the Secretary of State and Natural England to secure a route around the whole of the English coast consisting of one or more long-distance routes and available to the public for recreational journeys on foot or by ferry, together with public access rights to a wider area of land along the way for people to enjoy. In respect of land forming part of a proposed long-distance coastal route, s.3A also makes provision for that land not to become coastal margin until the end of an "access preparation period" in relation to the land. A number of Orders have been made under s.3A specifying the expiry of an "access preparation period" for various sections of long-distance coast paths. See, by way of example, the Access to the Countryside (Coastal Margin) (Weymouth Bay) Order 2012/1559.

Regulations. Where any other person holds a leasehold interest in the land, the dedication must be made jointly.[32]

4.5 S.15 specifies a number of enactments under which land is to be treated as accessible by members of the public for the purposes of s.1(1). These include metropolitan commons,[33] and public access to monuments under public control under s.19 of the Ancient Monuments and Archaeological Areas Act 1979.[34]

## Excepted or excluded land

4.6 Part 1 to Schedule 1 CROW 2000 sets out, by way of description, land which is excepted from the right to roam conferred by Part 1 of the Act. These exceptions include:

- i Land on which the soil has, in the last 12 months, been disturbed by ploughing or drilling for the purpose of planting or sowing crops or trees (other than, in England, land which is coastal margin or forms part of the coastal route strip)[35];
- ii Land covered by buildings, or the curtilage of such land;[36]
- iii Land within 20m of a dwelling (other than coastal margin in England);[37] and
- iv Land within a park or garden.[38]

---

32 S.16(2)

33 Pursuant to s.193 of the Law of Property Act 1925

34 For example, the scheduled ancient monuments in Dartmoor National Park. See paragraph 3.14 above.

35 Schedule 1 Part 1 paragraph 1

36 Schedule 1 Part 1 paragraph 2

37 Schedule 1 Part 1 paragraph 3

38 Schedule 1 Part 1 paragraph 4

4.7 The descriptions in Part 1 of Schedule 1 must be read with the definitions, and qualifications, contained in Part 2 of Schedule 2. For example, land habitually used for the training of race horses[39] is only to be treated as excepted land (a) between dawn and midday and (b) at any other time when it is use for that purpose.[40] Notably, land which would be excepted land by reference to development which had been carried out on it,[41] is not to be treated as excepted land if planning permission was required for that development[42] and has not been granted, unless the development is to be treated as lawful under s.191 of the TCPA 1990.[43]

## Conclusive maps

4.8 S.4(1) of CROW 2000 imposed a duty on Natural England to prepare maps showing all registered common land and all open country for England (outside Inner London).[44] The same duty applied to the Natural Resources Body for Wales in respect of land in Wales.[45] They were required to publish draft maps for consultation; to have regard to any representations received within the prescribed period regarding land shown (or not shown) as registered common land or open country on the draft map;, and to issue the map in provisional form (with or without modifications).[46]

4.9 In preparing a map under s.4 Natural England or the Natural Resources Body for Wales ("NRBW") may decide not to show as

[39] Schedule 1 Part 1 paragraph 12

[40] Schedule 1 Part 2 paragraph 17

[41] For example, land covered by buildings.

[42] Under Part III of the Town and Country Planning Act 1990

[43] Schedule 1 Part 2 paragraph 15.

[44] CROW s.4(1)

[45] CROW s.4(2).

[46] S.5

open country areas of land which they consider to be so small that there would be no useful purpose in including them.[47]

4.10 There is a right of appeal for any person having an interest in land shown on the map in its provisional form to the Secretary of State (for land in England) and to the National Assembly for Wales (for land in Wales).[48] An appeal may be brought only on the grounds that:

i Land shown as registered common land is not common land;[49]

ii Land shown as open country does not consist wholly or predominantly of mountain, moor, heath or down and, to the extent that the Natural England or the Natural Resources Board for Wales has exercised their discretion under s.4(5)(b) to treat land which is not open country as forming part of an area of open country, it should not have done so.[50]

4.11 An appeal may take the form of a hearing or inquiry.[51] The Secretary of State, or National Assembly for Wales, may confirm the map with or without modification, or require Natural England, or the Natural Resources Body for Wales, to prepare a new map for all or part of the area covered by the map at issue.[52]

4.12 Where the time for bringing an appeal has expired, or every appeal brought in relation to a map has been determined or with-

---

47 R (on the application of the Litmore Shaw Nature Trust) v The Countryside Agency [2005] EWHC 2050 (Admin) per HHJ Rich QC at para 5.

48 S.6(1)

49 S.6(2)

50 S.6(3)

51 S.7(1). S.250(2)-(5) of the Local Government Act 1972 apply, with modifications: s.7(2).

52 S.6(4)

drawn, the map is to be issued in conclusive form.[53] Natural England and the Natural Resources Body for Wales are under a duty to review the maps "from time to time", the first review to be undertaken after not more than 20 years (in England) and 10 years (in Wales).[54] The first review commenced in Wales in 2012, with revised conclusive maps published in 2014. The review of the open access maps was due to take place between 2019 and 2020 in England, but this will now take place between 2024 and 2025 to align with progress of the English coastal path.[55]

## The nature of the right under Part 1 CROW 2000

4.13 The right conferred on members of the public under Part 1 of CROW 2000 is the right to use access land on foot for recreation. Save with the agreement of the landowner, it does not include the right to (inter alia):

- i Drive or ride a vehicle, bicycle or horse[56];
- ii Bring an animal, other than a dog;[57]
- iii Camp[58];
- iv Engage in any commercial activity[59]; or
- v Without reasonable excuse, interfere with any fence, barrier or other device designed to enclose livestock, or neglect to shut or fasten any gate where any

---

53 S.9

54 S.10

55 https://www.gov.uk/guidance/open-access-land-management-rights-and-responsibilities#review-of-open-access-maps

56 Schedule 2, paragraphs 1(a) and (c)

57 Schedule 2, paragraph 1(c)

58 Schedule 2, paragraph 1(s)

59 Schedule 2, paragraph 1(t)

means of doing so is provided, unless it is reasonable to assume it is to be left open.[60]

4.14 The right to access land for the purpose of open-air recreation is also subject to the general conditions specified in s.2 of CROW 2000. In summary, a person may enter and remain on land as long as he does not break or damage any wall, fence, hedge, stile or gate;[61] he observes the general restrictions in Schedule 2 (examples of which are set out above);[62] he observes any other restrictions imposed on the land under Chapter II of CROW 2000;[63] and subject to any relevant 'statutory prohibition'.[64] A person who does not comply with those conditions becomes a trespasser, and may not exercise the rights conferred by s.2(1) to enter that land, or other land in the same ownership, for 72 hours.[65]

4.15 An "access authority" – being a National Park Authority or a highway authority – may make byelaws in respect of access land in their area, with contravention being punishable by fine.[66] Access to land may be restricted by direction of the "relevant authority"[67] pursuant to the powers conferred under Chapter II of CROW 2000.[68] Natural England and the NRBW also issue

60 Schedule 2, paragraphs 1(n) and (o).

61 CROW s.2(1)(a)

62 CROW s.2(1)(b)

63 CROW s.2(1)(b)

64 CROW s.2(3) & (3A)

65 CROW s.4

66 S.17

67 Natural England (in relation to any land which is coastal margin), the National Park Authority (for any land, other than coastal margin, in a National Park), the Forestry Commission (for woodland in England, where it has served notice on what would otherwise be the relevant authority), and otherwise the appropriate countryside body.

68 A relevant authority may, for example, make a direction excluding or restricting access to land during a specified period where satisfied that it is necessary for the

guidance on the use of access land under s.20 CROW 2000. Copies of the "Countryside Code" can be found on their websites.[69]

## 5 OWNERS RIGHTS AND LIABILITIES

5.1 Unless the landowner does something which gives rise to a risk of danger with the intention of creating that risk, or being reckless as to whether a risk is created, the landowner will not be liable under the Occupiers Liability Act 1984 in respect of:

i A risk resulting from the existence of any natural feature of the landscape, or any river, stream, ditch or pond (whether a natural feature or not); or

ii A risk of a person suffering injury when passing over, under or through any wall, fence or gate, except by proper use of the gate or stile.[70]

5.2 The owner of land consisting of moor managed for breeding and shooting grouse may provide that dogs are not to be brought onto land during a specified period, where necessary in connection with the management of land for that purpose.[71] A similar power is conferred to restrict dogs being brought onto

---

purpose of management of that land: s.24 CROW 2000. .Such a direction may be made on application by the landowner, or, in respect of coastal margin, without such application being made. A similar power is conferred by s. 26 where the relevant authority is satisfied that exclusion or restriction of access is necessary for the purpose of nature conservation or preservation of heritage assets. sS.27 vc.ontains general provisions in respect of such directions, and further provisions are contained in the Access to the Countryside (Exclusions and Restrictions) (England) Regulations 2003; Countryside Access (Exclusion or Restriction of Access) (Wales) Regulations 2003.

69 https://www.gov.uk/government/publications/the-countryside-code ; https://naturalresources.wales/days-out/the-countryside-codes/?lang=en

70 S.6A Occupiers Liability Act 1984.

71 S.23(1) CROW 2000

land for specified periods in connection with lambing.[72] A landowner may also exclude or restrict access to land on one or more days specified in the notice, not exceeding 28 days in any calendar year, provided he has given notice to the relevant authority in accordance with the relevant Regulations,[73] or requested a relevant authority to make a direction restricting access for a longer period.[74] In this context, a person "restricts" access where he provides that the right conferred by s.2(1) CROW is exercisable only:

- i along specified routes or ways;
- ii after entering the land at a specified place or places;
- iii by persons who do not take dogs on the land; or
- iv by persons who satisfy any other specified conditions.[75]

5.3 A landowner may not, however, place a notice on or near access land containing false or misleading information likely to deter the public from exercising their 'right to roam' on access land. Placing such a notice is an office, punishable by fine on summary conviction.[76]

---

72 S.23(2)

73 Access to the Countryside (Exclusions and Restrictions) (England) Regulations 2003; Countryside Access (Exclusion or Restriction of Access) (Wales) Regulations 2003.

74 See paragraph 4.15

75 S.21(3)

76 S.14

# INDEX

# MORE BOOKS BY LAW BRIEF PUBLISHING

A selection of our other titles available now:-

| |
|---|
| 'Covid-19, Homeworking and the Law – The Essential Guide to Employment and GDPR Issues' by Forbes Solicitors |
| 'Covid-19, Force Majeure and Frustration of Contracts – The Essential Guide' by Keith Markham |
| 'Covid-19 and Criminal Law – The Essential Guide' by Ramya Nagesh |
| 'Covid-19 and Family Law in England and Wales – The Essential Guide' by Safda Mahmood |
| 'Covid-19 and the Implications for Planning Law – The Essential Guide' by Bob Mc Geady & Meyric Lewis |
| 'Covid-19, Residential Property, Equity Release and Enfranchisement – The Essential Guide' by Paul Sams and Louise Uphill |
| 'Covid-19, Brexit and the Law of Commercial Leases – The Essential Guide' by Mark Shelton |
| 'Covid-19 and the Law Relating to Food in the UK and Republic of Ireland – The Essential Guide' by Ian Thomas |
| 'A Practical Guide to the General Data Protection Regulation (GDPR) – 2nd Edition' by Keith Markham |
| 'Ellis on Credit Hire – Sixth Edition' by Aidan Ellis & Tim Kevan |
| 'A Practical Guide to Working with Litigants in Person and McKenzie Friends in Family Cases' by Stuart Barlow |
| 'Protecting Unregistered Brands: A Practical Guide to the Law of Passing Off' by Lorna Brazell |
| 'A Practical Guide to Secondary Liability and Joint Enterprise Post-Jogee' by Joanne Cecil & James Mehigan |

| |
|---|
| 'A Practical Guide to the Pre-Action RTA Claims Protocol for Personal Injury Lawyers' by Antonia Ford |
| 'A Practical Guide to Neighbour Disputes and the Law' by Alexander Walsh |
| 'A Practical Guide to Forfeiture of Leases' by Mark Shelton |
| 'A Practical Guide to Coercive Control for Legal Practitioners and Victims' by Rachel Horman |
| 'A Practical Guide to Rights Over Airspace and Subsoil' by Daniel Gatty |
| 'Tackling Disclosure in the Criminal Courts – A Practitioner's Guide' by Narita Bahra QC & Don Ramble |
| 'A Practical Guide to the Law of Driverless Cars – Second Edition' by Alex Glassbrook, Emma Northey & Scarlett Milligan |
| 'A Practical Guide to TOLATA Claims' by Greg Williams |
| 'Artificial Intelligence – The Practical Legal Issues' by John Buyers |
| 'A Practical Guide to the Law of Prescription in Scotland' by Andrew Foyle |
| 'A Practical Guide to the Construction and Rectification of Wills and Trust Instruments' by Edward Hewitt |
| 'A Practical Guide to the Law of Bullying and Harassment in the Workplace' by Philip Hyland |
| 'How to Be a Freelance Solicitor: A Practical Guide to the SRA-Regulated Freelance Solicitor Model' by Paul Bennett |
| 'A Practical Guide to Prison Injury Claims' by Malcolm Johnson |
| 'A Practical Guide to the Small Claims Track' by Dominic Bright |
| 'A Practical Guide to Advising Clients at the Police Station' by Colin Stephen McKeown-Beaumont |
| 'A Practical Guide to Antisocial Behaviour Injunctions' by Iain Wightwick |
| 'Practical Mediation: A Guide for Mediators, Advocates, Advisers, Lawyers, and Students in Civil, Commercial, Business, Property, Workplace, and Employment Cases' by Jonathan Dingle with John Sephton |
| 'The Mini-Pupillage Workbook' by David Boyle |

| |
|---|
| 'A Practical Guide to Crofting Law' by Brian Inkster |
| 'A Practical Guide to Spousal Maintenance' by Liz Cowell |
| 'A Practical Guide to the Law of Domain Names and Cybersquatting' by Andrew Clemson |
| 'A Practical Guide to the Law of Gender Pay Gap Reporting' by Harini Iyengar |
| 'A Practical Guide to the Rights of Grandparents in Children Proceedings' by Stuart Barlow |
| 'NHS Whistleblowing and the Law' by Joseph England |
| 'Employment Law and the Gig Economy' by Nigel Mackay & Annie Powell |
| 'A Practical Guide to Noise Induced Hearing Loss (NIHL) Claims' by Andrew Mckie, Ian Skeate, Gareth McAloon |
| 'An Introduction to Beauty Negligence Claims – A Practical Guide for the Personal Injury Practitioner' by Greg Almond |
| 'Intercompany Agreements for Transfer Pricing Compliance' by Paul Sutton |
| 'Zen and the Art of Mediation' by Martin Plowman |
| 'A Practical Guide to the SRA Principles, Individual and Law Firm Codes of Conduct 2019 – What Every Law Firm Needs to Know' by Paul Bennett |
| 'A Practical Guide to Adoption for Family Lawyers' by Graham Pegg |
| 'A Practical Guide to Industrial Disease Claims' by Andrew Mckie & Ian Skeate |
| 'A Practical Guide to Redundancy' by Philip Hyland |
| 'A Practical Guide to Vicarious Liability' by Mariel Irvine |
| 'A Practical Guide to Applications for Landlord's Consent and Variation of Leases' by Mark Shelton |
| 'A Practical Guide to Relief from Sanctions Post-Mitchell and Denton' by Peter Causton |
| 'A Practical Guide to Equity Release for Advisors' by Paul Sams |
| 'A Practical Guide to Unlawful Eviction and Harassment' by Stephanie Lovegrove |
| 'A Practical Guide to the Law Relating to Food' by Ian Thomas |

'A Practical Guide to Financial Services Claims' by Chris Hegarty

'The Law of Houses in Multiple Occupation: A Practical Guide to HMO Proceedings' by Julian Hunt

'A Practical Guide to Unlawful Eviction and Harassment' by Stephanie Lovegrove

'A Practical Guide to Solicitor and Client Costs' by Robin Dunne

'Occupiers, Highways and Defective Premises Claims: A Practical Guide Post-Jackson – 2nd Edition' by Andrew Mckie

'A Practical Guide to Financial Ombudsman Service Claims' by Adam Temple & Robert Scrivenor

'A Practical Guide to Advising Schools on Employment Law' by Jonathan Holden

'A Practical Guide to Running Housing Disrepair and Cavity Wall Claims: 2nd Edition' by Andrew Mckie & Ian Skeate

'A Practical Guide to Holiday Sickness Claims – 2nd Edition' by Andrew Mckie & Ian Skeate

'Arguments and Tactics for Personal Injury and Clinical Negligence Claims' by Dorian Williams

'A Practical Guide to QOCS and Fundamental Dishonesty' by James Bentley

'A Practical Guide to Drone Law' by Rufus Ballaster, Andrew Firman, Eleanor Clot

'A Practical Guide to Compliance for Personal Injury Firms Working With Claims Management Companies' by Paul Bennett

'A Practical Guide to the Landlord and Tenant Act 1954: Commercial Tenancies' by Richard Hayes & David Sawtell

'A Practical Guide to Dog Law for Owners and Others' by Andrea Pitt

'RTA Allegations of Fraud in a Post-Jackson Era: The Handbook – 2nd Edition' by Andrew Mckie

'RTA Personal Injury Claims: A Practical Guide Post-Jackson' by Andrew Mckie

'On Experts: CPR35 for Lawyers and Experts' by David Boyle

'An Introduction to Personal Injury Law' by David Boyle

| 'A Practical Guide to Chronic Pain Claims' by Pankaj Madan |
|---|
| 'A Practical Guide to Claims Arising from Fatal Accidents' by James Patience |
| 'A Practical Guide to Subtle Brain Injury Claims' by Pankaj Madan |

www.ingramcontent.com/pod-product-compliance
Lightning Source LLC
LaVergne TN
LVHW052306200926
848481LV00002B/485